The Romantic Dimension

The Romantic Dimension

JANE OTIENO

XULON PRESS

Xulon Press
2301 Lucien Way #415
Maitland, FL 32751
407.339.4217
www.xulonpress.com

© 2021 by Jane Otieno
Tribute to Joseph Otieno

All rights reserved solely by the author. The author guarantees all contents are original and do not infringe upon the legal rights of any other person or work. No part of this book may be reproduced in any form without the permission of the author. The views expressed in this book are not necessarily those of the publisher.

Due to the changing nature of the Internet, if there are any web addresses, links, or URLs included in this manuscript, these may have been altered and may no longer be accessible. The views and opinions shared in this book belong solely to the author and do not necessarily reflect those of the publisher. The publisher therefore disclaims responsibility for the views or opinions expressed within the work.

Unless otherwise indicated, Scripture quotations taken from the New King James Version (NKJV). Copyright © 1982 by Thomas Nelson, Inc. Used by permission. All rights reserved.

Paperback ISBN-13: 978-1-6628-3192-8
Ebook ISBN-13: 978-1-6628-3193-5

Dedication

This book is dedicated to my husband Joseph, without whom I would have never known the joy of romantic love.

Table of Contents

Foreword ix

Love Power 1
Investment in Value 3
From Eternity Past 9
Choosing Love 13
Attributes Of Love 15
Choosing Selfihness 17
The Origin Of Romance 21
Echos From Eden 25
The Human Tragedy 27
Romantic Love Peaks 29
From This Day Forward 31
Spiritual Dimension of Love 33
Romantic Influence On Human Life 35
Nature of Love 37
Interpersonal Relationships 45
Needs A Man In Marrieage 47
What Women Expect in Marriage 51

The Romantic dimension

How Romantic Love Flows................................55
Stumbling blocks to love flow........................57
An Epic Love Story 61
Jacob's Love For Rachel................................63
Marriages of convenience.............................65
The Triumph of Love...................................69
The Holiness Of Sex....................................71
Why Sexual Security Is Good For Your Well-Being.....79
Walking The Narrow Way..............................91
Covenant Marriage 97
Conflict Resolution 105
Unfaithfulness..109
Breakups 113
Love Companionship 117
Love and Faith..121

Foreword

EVERYONE HAS THEIR own love story no matter where you are in life.

No matter where you are in life, you need love. You could be a famous personality in political arenas, a famous athlete, or someone in entertainment industry, a public figure in society or just an ordinary person, and still your heart yearns to be loved by that one person you value most. You want to go to that person every time you go back home. That person is your home. You want that person to be there when you win the trophies and when you have been beaten and defeated. Your heart yearns for their approval. You want their love only. That person influences your Spiritual wellbeing. The cheers and the love from your fans, friends, and close relatives cannot replace the admiration, adoration, and love from that person is paramount.

You could live in a mansion, but without the love of that person your joy is void. You could be a household name in your country or the whole world, but you want to hear their voice say, "I Love you". Their words soak and saturate your heart with hope when you feel like your world is falling apart. Falling in love and living in that love is possible. It is what all of us need.

The highest achievement is being able to love and receive love.

Love Power

EVERY HUMAN HEART yearns for love. In everything we do, if and when love is not the motivating factor disappointment and pain is inevitable.

Love is the driving power of good. Love must be received and must be given time to grow once planted in someone's heart. Rejecting love and the failure to love are causes of human tragedy on planet earth. I have looked around and have tried to find the meaning of life and what makes humans happy and joyful. I have looked around and have tried to find what makes humans experience a feeling of satisfaction and accomplishment. I could not find one single factor that makes one human full of joy. But, whoever finds love and passion can testify that love gives meaning to life. Even though humans are selfish by nature, love still has the greatest impact on our lives. The majority of humans are born out of a love relationship and even those who are not still have the desire to love and to be loved. And those who come from loving homes, more often than not, will develop a positive outlook on life because someone loved them in their childhood.

Millions of artists in all languages, cultures, and races all over the world sing about love, even when their own lifestyle is marred with selfishness. Love can indeed rear its beautiful head in unfamiliar places.

The Romantic Dimension

King Solomon, the son of King David, wrote a masterpiece of romantic love in the Bible book called the Song of Solomon. Yet, he violated the principle of true love by marrying a thousand wives. However, he did not leave this planet before he recognized the power and the beauty of love. At the end of his life, he realized the folly of living in selfishness and wrote in Ecclesiastes 9:9, "Enjoy life with the woman of your youth." Solomon missed the intimacy of loving one woman after his escapades with many wives. He learned hard lessons from his marital mistakes and wrote it down for you and me so that we would not have to walk down that treacherous path.

The fact that humans can sing, write, and preach love and yet live selfish lives like King Solomon and many people today is a strong indication that love is not a human creation or idea. Love is a Divine Principle. The Bible says in 1 John 8 "God is Love." God is the foundation of all types of love. His kingdom is based on the foundation of love.

Those who allow themselves to be loved by God can truly love now and forever. God is love and when we accept that we are loved by Him, we become a channel of love. We can love because we have been loved.

This principle of love does not just apply to being able to love because of the love of God. . Those who have been loved by parents, siblings, friends, and spouses can love because they have been loved. The greatest gift and legacy we can leave to our spouses, children, siblings, friends, and everyone around us is love.

Love empowers people to treat others well even at their own loss. Love is the greatest force in the whole universe. Love lasts forever.

It is not a coincidence that a romantic love song is placed in the middle of the Bible in the Song of Solomon. It is God's providential plan for all humans to learn about love.

God's Kingdom is based on the principle of love. When you love someone, they become valuable and precious to you. Anything that you value in your life becomes important to you. You invest time and money in what you value.

Investment in Value

MANY PEOPLE INVEST their wealth where they believe they will earn profits. When investing wealth in financial institutions, there are risks that come with these investments. One of the biggest risks is loss. Loving someone comes with a risk of pain and loss.

To make a marriage work, you must value the relationship enough to invest time and devotion, sacrificing your wants and sometimes your needs in order for the marriage to be successful. Many people sacrifice relationships for money, pleasure, and convenience. You cannot reap what you did not sow. When you plan to invest your emotions, time, and yourself in someone, you better take time to know them well enough to warrant your devotion to them.

One way of building a strong marital foundation is to postpone sexual intimacy until permanent commitment is determined in marriage vows.

In order to let the relationship mature, postpone sexual intimacy as it is the climax of a romantic relationship. You cannot climb a ladder from the top, you climb from the bottom as you go up. Self-control in sexual intimacy does not begin with marriage: it begins before you commit to love someone. Self-control is a virtue that safeguards

The Romantic dimension

relationships. When you practice self-control, you are investing yourself in a relationship. Self-control does not just involve sexuality; it helps in checking anger, impulsive outbursts, impulsive shopping, gluttony, and many other extreme behaviors which impede relationships.

Another way you can invest yourself in a relationship by caring for your health for the sake of your partner. When a woman wants to get pregnant, she watches what she eats for the sake of the baby. She stops smoking, drinking alcohol, and makes sure her lifestyle does not harm the growing fetus in her womb. This is called maternal love. It is important to look good, smell good, and to be attractive. Loving yourself is a strong and mature way of loving your partner. If you expect your partner to do the same, then lead the way.

You invest money in your relationship by providing for your family.

Sometimes family can face difficulty earning enough money to cater for their needs in general depending on the economic condition of a country or state. The bad economy is no excuse to not invest money into the relationship. When you love someone, you do not just give them your body, time, and heart but you share your possessions with them as a gesture of kindness and care.

The Issue of money and material wealth is a sensitive topic when it comes to marital relationships. However, handling finances with wisdom deliberately and conscientiously is key to avoiding pitfalls in marital relationships. Money should not be the basis for a relationship. Money only buys stuff and material comfort. Money cannot make you love someone, or make them love you. Money cannot change one's bad behaviors, habits, or character. Distinctions between someone being attracted to you to your money sometimes is a thin line. Time and situations often bring out true motives.

When you share material possessions, it should not be used as a bait to win someone's love for you. When you love someone, determine their commitment to you and to the relationship before you share material possessions.

Investment In Value

Since a lot of people get attracted to big beautiful houses, nice cars, fat bank accounts, and the influence of power that money brings with it, the person with material wealth and social influence ought to be wise and careful. While it is true money moves things, it hardly move hearts.

The truth is, everyone wants to have more money to buy more things and pay bills. But wisdom informs us that paying all our bills and buying all the stuff we need and want does not lead to happiness and contentment. There is more to life than buying material possessions and paying bills. There is a whole world of love and life out there. Money is something that should be used to bless human life, and love should be the reason to use money.

Everyone born on this planet wonders about the meaning and the purpose of living. When you want to know the truth about the reason for your existence, look to and study nature. Every living thing in nature exists for the benefit of others. Humans are the beneficiary of nature in general. Consider these examples:

a. Water exists to serve humanity. We drink it, wash ourselves and our clothes with it, and use water for irrigation and the production of goods, etc. All humans and many creatures would be dead without water.

b. The sun is light in the day, provides vitamin D for human health, solar energy, and is a source of life to plants and animals.

c. Trees, plants and all vegetation exist for the natural environment and for humanity. Environmentalists constantly remind us that when humans abuse and interfere with natural environments, humans, animals and all plants risk extinction.

The Romantic dimension

Living a whole life is living with the purpose to make the world around you a better place to live by loving and caring for people around you.

Happiness and contentment come by loving, giving and serving.

True Love that stands the test of time must be developed over time. You cannot fully love a stranger or someone you barely know. There is wonder and indescribable beauty in gazing into the eyes of your beloved and holding them with your heart, body, and mind. It is magical to hold them tight and feel their heart beat close. There is an unexplained mystery in how a romantic love between a man and woman works. There is no one method of falling in love. There is no right way or wrong way. Love warms the heart like a beautiful music that can lull you into a trance. Romantic love mesmerizes the human mind with goodness and beauty. The butterflies in the stomach are real before we turn them into caterpillars. Romantic love fills the heart with beautiful songs. No wonder we have more romantic songs than all other songs in the world.

Romantic love can be dangerous when not wisely handled. Many homicide cases are related to love affairs that have resulted in abortions, murders, divorce, love triangles, polygamy, bigamy, adultery, and fornication. All these painful ills can all be the results of underestimating the power of romantic love when misplaced, misunderstood, and misused.

Kings and great leaders have fallen from glory into shame through misplaced romantic love. The clergy and the saints both have reaped the folly of ignoring romantic love and by misplacing their affections.

The secular media displays the lie that sexuality is a base feeling founded on lust. Male and female body parts are displayed on magazines and in videos to encourage the masses to focus on appearance over substance of character.

The so called "music entertainment displays videos that demean and project female bodies as merchandise to be sold for the lusting eyes of the beholder. While projecting nudity and lewdness, love and decency are sacrificed on the altar of amusement.

Anyone who wants to escape the lure and the lies peddled by these lewd media sources of communication must endeavor to learn the truth and the meaning of Love. Love places value on the person, Lust and exploitation place value on the appearance and perception of the mind and the eyes. When you allow yourself to watch the bewitching videos that promote the base taste of lust, it is very hard to reason and see clearly what meaning of true love.

The reason young minds know so much about sex and so little about love is the fact that love does not sell, sex does. Rarely do you see videos about love, but instead sex is in commercials and advertised on billboards everywhere. For one to find love, they must dig deeper than what they see on the surface.

What you believe shapes your behavior. When you discover the true meaning of loving another human being, you acquire new lenses through which you look at a human being. True love removes scales of deceptions from our eyes. Seeking love is finding life.

Love is sacred and above the canal comprehension of the human mind. One needs a spiritual encounter with the Author of Love in order to truly immerse themselves in the beauty of love.

Love values life. Love protects life. Love preserves sexuality.

From Eternity Past

IN GENESIS CHAPTER 1, we read the account of how life on planet earth was created. The Creator of life on this planet had a plan. He created life to be enjoyed and appreciated by human beings. He created a paradise on planet earth and created lovers to enjoy living and appreciating His creation. He created Adam and Eve and married them. He gave them the world as their possession and empowered them to love each other.

The Creator gave Adam and Eve power to procreate. In other words, He empowered humans with His ability to create another human being, which originally was His own. But instead of creating each human, as he created Adam and Eve. He trusted that power to the human race.

The Creator gave Adam and Eve the power to rule over all the creatures on Earth

The Creator gave Adam the order of how their relationship would begin.

He said from that day forward, a man would leave his parents and cleave to his wife and become one flesh. Cleaving in this context means becoming one in purpose and agreement and becoming sexually intimate in a marriage covenant.

The Romantic dimension

In other words, leaving precedes cleaving, and cleaving precedes becoming one flesh. This order clears the confusion of how, when, and what to do concerning marital relationships and when sex should be involved in a relationship.

The Creator manifested His love by creating the world and putting life on it and went further to create a paradise and called it Eden. Then He created Adam and gave him everything and then He created Eve to help Adam enjoy life in that paradise.

The Creator then created two trees in the middle of the paradise. The Tree of Life and the Tree of Knowledge of Good and Evil side by side. By putting these two trees in the middle of paradise, the Creator did something that billions of people on planet earth do not understand. However, when you understand this act by the Creator then you will begin to see the glimpse of what happened to the perfect creation, what happened to Adam and Eve, and why our world is no longer a paradise but instead a war zone.

Adam and Eve were not created like robots who could be controlled by God Himself or by the Devil. They were created as free beings. They were free to choose to have a relationship with the very God who created them.

1. Yes, the Creator loved Adam and Eve and gave them the whole world. The Creator had to give Adam and Eve a choice to love Him back. They were free to choose the Tree of Life or the Tree of Knowledge of Good and Evil. That was the test of allegiance.

2. The Creator explained in details what would happen to the human family on the day they would decide to eat the fruit from the Tree of Knowledge of Good and Evil. They would die a spiritual death and ultimately a physical death as a result of choosing to eat from the second tree. We are not told how

many centuries Adam and Eve only ate fruit from the Tree of Life. But one day they both ate from the Tree of Knowledge of Good and Evil. Their choice brought damnation to the earth and to Adam's descendants. All humans born on planet earth suffer the consequences of our first ancestor's choice.

3. The story of the two trees in the middle of Eden's paradise is proof that we were created by the Creator with the freedom to determine your own fate. Freedom must have two alternative sides to choose. You choose your destiny. Both choices have consequences, both here and now and in eternity.

4. Since you now know that there are two sides of life to choose from, you must also learn what these two ways of life entail. One way is choosing love. The other way is choosing selfishness. When you decide to choose love, the first step is to recognize that you are loved. You accept to receive that love, and then apply that love to influence your relationships with others. Your passion, work ethic, and purpose for living become your joy. You desire to make a positive difference when given the opportunity to serve another human being. You can only give what you have received and possess. It is to believe that you were created for a higher purpose. You were created unique in the sense that no one on this planet can replace you as an individual. You have an assignment on earth.

You will discover your assignment when you begin to embrace love. Love is explained in the moral laws in the summary of the Ten Commandments which states that we all should treat one another the same way we want to be treated. Exodus 20; 12-17.
The law we see in nature teaches us to live to bless others the way trees serve humanity by producing oxygen for human existence. Water

The Romantic dimension

exists for human survival and the Sun exists for human wellbeing by providing sunlight and vitamin D. and also the sun aids plants to grow so we can use plants for food and more.

The more we look and study nature the more we learn from it on how we should live for one another to fulfil each other's needs.

Choosing Love

WHEN YOU HAVE the freedom to choose between two things, you have an advantage to choose between what you value most verses what you value least. Your choice would also depend on the information you believe about your preference. When you decide to choose love, it is important to know the value of love and what love entails. You will need to ask the fundamental questions like is the love you are choosing real or fake and what is love. The first step to choosing love is to know where love originated. If love is so important, you must know its source. The bible says, "God is Love"

The creator chose to create you. Out of millions of sperms produced by a man during fertilization only one sperm fertilizes the female egg. This means you do not randomly exist. You were chosen to be here by the Creator who is the Founder of love, marriage, and sexuality. Even though, your parents may have chosen each other, the Creator put everything in motion. He was expecting your arrival because He has great plans for you. He chose your unique features, your race, your height, your color, your DNA, and yes even your looks which are all unique and original. You are not a prototype of anyone. You are the only original you on this planet and He loves you because

The Romantic Dimension

you are His original masterpiece. He made only one you. Knowing your uniqueness is one step to loving yourself.

Loving yourself for whose you are and whose image you are created in, is the second step to accepting yourself for who you are. This moves you to another step which is valuing others as they are also unique in the eyes of the Creator God.

For you to love someone genuinely, you must first love yourself. You cannot give what you do not have. Knowing and accepting that God loves you gives you the ability to love and value another human being. The first step to a healthy marital relationship is falling in love with Love.

Because Adam and Eve chose selfishness, chaotic relationships in the human family were produced. Choosing love is not easy because selfishness always fights back through the forces of evil power, ignorance, and misinformation about Love.

Attributes Of Love

TRUE LOVE ALLOWS freedom of choice. When you love someone, you let them choose you. If they do not choose you, then honor their choice even at your loss. That is Divine love. God allowed Adam and Eve to choose the wrong fruit. Free will is the Creator's method of operation. For Him to restore order and hope for humanity, it cost Him His life. When you love someone, you set them free to choose you or to reject your love. That is Moral law of Love

True love does not make choices that harm other people. It is not self-centered. It is others centered. It practices the golden rule "Do unto others as you would like them do unto you" This Love is universal which means everybody needs to be loved regardless of race, tribe, language, or ethnicity.

Love sees the good in other people. Love appreciates the beauty, achievements, and success of other people even when your own life is full of failure and disappointments. Love does not envy. Love is not puffed up. Love promotes others.

Love is kind, patient, gentle, peaceful, joyful and beautiful. When you have this kind of love no one is threatened; they will rotate around your presence. This is infectious Love. It is bright and shines.

The Romantic dimension

Love is faithful. Love keeps the promise to always love no matter the circumstances. Love is the power of good in the middle of chaos and uncertainty. Faith gives love power to survive in unfamiliar circumstances.

1. Love is the most powerful force in the universe. Love conquers selfishness and hate. Love heals the wounded souls and love restores order. Love brings harmony in families torn apart by separations and hostility. Love forgives and restores broken relationships.

2. Love sacrifices ambitions, financial gain, and even life for the sake of others. Love gives the reason for your existence. Power, money and fame are something but love is everything.

Choosing Selfishness

The day Adam and Eve chose to eat the forbidden fruit, they demonstrated lack of trust in God who had given instructions against eating the forbidden fruit. And since God is the source of life, they disconnected the power line which resulted in their spiritual and physical death.

Whether informed or uninformed, your choice falls into two categories in this world; love or selfishness. It does not matter whether you are religious, an atheist, an animist, or a secular individual. We all chose one way or another. And your choice impacts not only your life, but your family, neighbors, strangers and people living in other countries, and even ones yet to be born.

Your choice impacts the lives of animals and the natural environment. Yes, our choices impacts other human beings, animals, and the natural world. Now you know that when our first ancestors chose to cut themselves from the source of love and life, their choice affected negatively all who are born on this planet. The moment we are born, we begin to degenerate the same day. In between the point of birth to the point of death, we struggle to survive because there are so many forces of evil around us with potential to kill us. From ravaging diseases, to accidents, to murderers, to self-inflicted deaths.

The Romantic dimension

While it is true that the consequences of the selfish choice of Adam and Eve still affects our world today, there is also the Force of Love side by side with the forces of evil. If there was no Force of Love among human beings, forces of evil would engulf us all and no one would be existing today. This is because The Creator God, provided a solution as soon as Adam and Eve cut themselves from Him. He came looking for them to give them a way out of death. He gave them another chance to choose love and to choose life. Jesus offered Himself as a sacrifice to redeem man from the disobedience to the Laws of love. Disobedience to the laws of God is called sin. Sin produces negative consequences in our relationship with God and people.

Jesus offers to give power over sin when we decide to trust God and His word. This is the Ultimate Love. You have that choice today too.

Jesus says in His word. "Love one another as I have loved you". He who does not love does not know God. For God is Love. His Love is everlasting. This Love is constant, faithful, and dependable. This is the foundation of love. (John 13.34)

Only love can forgive past mistakes and sin. Only love can heal us all from the ravages of sin and death. This is what God offers: healing love. When love possesses you, then and only then, are you able to love.

When you begin to love, you begin to truly live life to its fullest measure even though the world is not a perfect place. When you begin to love, you begin to be whole. You become whole in the spirit, mental, and physical functions of your body. Your spirit connects with the Holy Spirit, your mental focus begin to function on a higher level of reasoning, and your soul begins the service of love to humanity.

Love is the foundation of life. Anything you do can be influenced by it; your job, your ministry, your profession, your relationships with family, friends, neighbors and strangers. The most effective love is the one that is tested, tried, and shaken, yet still stands the test of time and negative circumstances.

Love will always go through trials. Love will be tried when you are tempted to compromise the truth. When you are tempted to sacrifice the wellbeing of the people you love for other things like fame, wealth etc., and love will be tempted when you compromise your sexual morality for temporary pleasures. As long as you live, you will be required to preserve Love by refusing compromises.

When you claim to love God, it must be manifest in how you treat people. When you value people over your wants and needs, then that is how you love God. Anyone who hurts another human being in the form of slavery, oppression, and all forms of abuse committed in the name of power, religion or authority cannot claim to love God. He who treats one human being with dignity even when that person is a criminal can claim to know God.

The tragic violence involving love affairs and subsequent break ups in families all over the world today is a result of rejecting true love and its principles and source

When a person learns what it takes to love another human being, they become careful on how to handle a relationship. Marital relationships are complex. Love untangles the web of confusion and falsehood. Those who seek love, expose themselves to Divine power.

The Origin Of Romance

GOD CREATED A man and a woman to complement each other in relationship, in their nature, and physique. Gen 2; 18-25 Man is physically rugged and strong. His masculine nature is meant to complement a woman's feminine nature of delicate beauty.

God created a handsome man and fashioned a beautiful woman.

God created the world and made a paradise for Adam and Eve to live in. Before Eve was created for Adam, God had given Adam dominion over the whole world with everything in it. So when Eve was created, Adam owned the whole world. Man is the custodian of the material well-being of the family. The woman was the co-inheritor of the material world at the beginning of creation.

At creation, the woman was given the ability to bear children while the man was given the responsibility to care for the material world. In order for the union of a man and a woman to sustain their family, they need a unique kind of relationship called romantic love.

Adam was created with a void in his heart that could only be filled by a woman. That is why, after Adam named everything created, he nevertheless felt lonely as the material world could not fill the void in his heart. Then God acknowledged Adam's loneliness and said, "It is not good for man to be alone, I will create for him a helpmeet." This

The Romantic dimension

means God created a woman to complement or meet the need of a man that he could not fulfill on his own. It also means the man was also created to meet the needs of a woman that she could not meet or fulfill by herself. In other words, both man and woman need each other in marriage.

God created a woman out of a rib He took from Adam after putting him to sleep. This could not have been a normal sleep. I believe it symbolized death. Adam was to die or become unconscious for God to remove one of his ribs to create a woman. God could have created a woman the same way He created a man, but he did not do that. He made a woman out of a man to cement the unique relationship between a husband and a wife. There is a real, unique connection between a husband and wife that the human brain cannot fathom without spiritual revelation. It is a divine spiritual connection of its own kind.

Adam saw Eve, beaming with beauty and a semblance of himself, and he could not help himself but overcome with love at first sight and composed a poem. "This is bone of my bones and flesh of my flesh, and she shall be called woman." This is the first romantic affair on planet earth. Adam and Eve lived in paradise and were happy until they chose a different path from their creator's plans.

This is the account given in the Bible as the beginning of love, marriage, and family. It is the most credible account of human origin. The fact that a human being was created in the image of the Creator of the Universe and that God created a woman out of a man and empowered them to be able to procreate by an act that involves love and bears children that look like them is a powerful message to humanity. Humans are valuable to the Creator. He created humans in His image and gave them the power to create in their image. This sounds like the Creator extended the family tree from Himself to humans. He extended His kingdom to humans by giving them the love principles to live by. This is why the only principle that works on planet earth is love, because it is the manual from the Manufacturer of the World and the people in it. Couples who want to succeed in marriage should follow the instructions from the Master Designer.

The belief that humans came from evolution is designed to reduce human value to a mere biological union of sperm and egg. Those who promote these kinds of teachings cannot promote the idea and the principle of love. Love comes from the Creator God and that love puts value on every human life. When one claims to worship that God, he must be able to love, because God is love.

Echos From Eden

The day God married Adam and Eve in paradise (Eden), Adam said these eternal words, "From this day forward, a man shall leave his parents and cleave to his wife and they shall be one flesh." They were one flesh indeed biologically.

Before Eve was created, Adam has access to the whole material world but he was alone. He needed someone with whom to enjoy sightseeing the beauty of the world. Someone to share meals with, someone to have conversations with, to laugh with, to play with, and to share thoughts and decisions with. In other words, Adam needed a companion.

Adam needed someone to love and with whom to share intimacy. That person was Eve.

Romantic love is God's idea. He planned the institution of marriage from the beginning of Creation. Loving someone and marrying them is a spiritual undertaking.

Adam needed a romantic lover and a sexual partner. God provided one. Humans are social beings by nature. They were created to need and live with each other for companionship and for fulfilment of each other's needs.

The Romantic dimension

God the Creator of the Universe and people on planet earth, introduced love, marriage and family.

Therefore, when you love someone and treat them with the dignity, it makes them joyful and fulfilled. You are actually honoring the Creator.

Loving someone is loving God indirectly because God is the creator of the person you love. When you love, you honor God.

You honor the parents of your spouse by treating them with respect and honor because they brought him/her into this world.

Those who honor their vows and promises will enjoy their married lives. But those who do not care about the principles of a married relationship, bring pain and tragedy to themselves and to others.

When a couple believes that they are brought together by Divine providence, they are likely to honor each other knowing God is supreme in their relationship. They will seek the principles of that Creator to guide them in their relationship. Just like when you buy a car, it comes with a manual for maintenance. God the Author of love, marriage, and family protects and defends the family when He is invited to the union.

The Human Tragedy

GENESIS CHAPTER 3 records the twist to the happily ever after in the story of our first parents' love affair. Eve was deceived into eating the forbidden fruit by an unsuspected enemy who lived around them and she convinced Adam to eat the same fruit. By disobeying the clear command of God their Creator, they chose to disconnect themselves from the source of blessings. Due to guilt, they both ran away from God when He came to visit them in the Garden. But God's love sought them out to give them a promise of His love despite their disobedience.

In their fallen nature, their love for each other was dented when Adam blamed Eve for his disobedience and blamed God for creating him a wife. Eve blamed the snake . They both blamed God. Sin entered the world through deception. Deception about love and life is predominant with humans and that is why we must seek the truth to be free.

God pronounced the consequences of their choices and pronounced doom to the snake's family, which symbolized Satan, for deceiving Eve. Adam and Eve lost their paradise and life on planet earth has never been as God intended it to be. God provided a way out of sin by providing a Savior who would take away their sin by repentance and reconciliation to God. That day a lamb died. The lamb symbolized Christ.

Adam and Eve were given a second chance to make it right. However, because of their fallen nature, their son Cain was born with a sinful nature who due to envy, murdered his younger brother Abel. Our first ancestors' married life was never the same. They were forgiven for their sins, but they acquired a sinful nature. And sin destroys human joy and peace.

This is our story. We are born in sin. This is why those who do not adhere to the principles of love as designed by the Creator God, hurt others due to selfishness. Selfishness is a sin.

When we want to be happy, we must make others happy. If we would do this, the world of love, marriage, and family would not suffer the violence and betrayals as witnessed in our generation today.

We need to go back to the drawing board and seek the principles of love in order to live with a purpose. Marriages do not break, they are broken.

Romantic Love Peaks

AN IDEAL PERFECT wedding is described as follows;
A Bride walks down the aisle of the church majestically with grace and style, all eyes are on the bride, dressed in pure white bedecked with silver lace. Her cheeks are round and youthful. Her calculated steps are admirable and the girls in the audience are looking forward to this day. Every young woman has this dream of wearing the white gown and walking on the arm of her father to be presented as a gift to her Prince Charming. It is the bride's day and everyone is happy for her and of course for him. The air is pregnant with love, laughter, and happiness. The bride's mother is in tears and everyone assumes it is tears of happiness; of course, who would think otherwise.

The vows are exchanged. The groom means it as he lovingly, with his deep voice, looks into her eyes and boldly tells her, "I hereby take thee to be my wedded wife to love thee for better, for worse, for richer, for poorer till death do us part." His hands are trembling with passion; his body is full of sensual desires. He kisses the bride's lips. The bride repeats the same vows as she is overwhelmed with romantic emotions and joy beyond expression fills her heart. She feels like she is going to faint, but the groom is holding her tight. They are declared husband and wife.

The Romantic dimension

The audience nods their heads in approval, the women shout for joy. Everyone blesses the couple with gifts, songs, dances, and speeches. The music is so serene and full of endearing words.

Then there is prayer, a long kiss, the ring, the songs, the dances, the cake, the food, the limousines, and the honeymoon.

Then married life begins.

Weddings are lovely occasions that many people love to attend. Each time I attend a wedding my happiness climbs to the roof. I believe I am not the only one feeling dizzy with joy. I sincerely never forget to say prayers to Almighty God to help the couple realize the seriousness of their vows, and to be able to overcome future challenges ahead.

Most young women dream of a beautiful romantic wedding and to live happily ever after.

While the statistics show high divorce rates in many modern cities, people of all walks of life still yearn for true love. Love gives people hope.

Break ups and divorce have not stopped people from falling in love and getting married. Love still wins even when relationships fail.

People may fail each other, but love will never fail. It is planted in young and old hearts every day.

Those who divorce and separate still yearn and look for love. It is the only way to survive. Therefore, divorce will hurt people but cannot kill the quest for love.

People will betray each other but love will never betray people.

People will trample on love, but love will survive and march on.

Love is beautiful, strong, and resilient. We need to believe in love no matter the past hurt. It is the only way to live.

From This Day Forward

WEDDINGS ARE DONE in one day, but marriage is every day for life. Couples mean well when they say their vows before the church and God. It is wise for couples to make sure they both know the foundation on which to build their marriage vows. Weddings are beautiful occasions that leave long-lasting good memories for the couple and for all in attendance. But love can only survive on a firm foundation of sacrifice, faith, trust and commitment. Memories are good but when couples fail to continue making good memories with each other after the honeymoon, their lives can be marred with resentment, passivity, and total neglect of each other's needs for affection and attention.

Couples ought to learn from the failure of others by decluttering their lives from unnecessary traditions that put more burdens on their time with each other, finances, and the foundation of their love.

Each wedding tells its own story, and each person has a story that is brought to the altar of their marriage. It could be a true sincere love story built over years of perseverance and challenges. It could be innocence of youth and passion. Or it could be the past affairs and broken promises and dreams. It could be the fierce determination to love no matter what happens in the future.

The Romantic Dimension

All the past issues need to be addressed before the wedding.

Marital counseling is needed prior to the wedding, if one went through any kind of abuse like violence, abandonment, rape, and any type of trauma including accidents.

On the wedding day, few care about the stability of the union as much as they care about the dress, the cake, the food, and yes, all the glamour and styles. Most young women pay attention to details about the glitter and the glamour of the event of a wedding. Decorations, flower arrangements, guests' food, and limousines become the focus. At times this goes for men who foot the wedding bills, or get into debt trying to impress friends and relatives.

Wise couples will make sure they pay attention to their relationship and build a lasting foundation that will sustain their union against spending fortunes to impress people who care little about their happiness.

Planning for a lavish wedding, if you can afford it, without getting into debt is good since you only have one wedding with that person in this life. But getting into debt to have a lavish wedding is not wise. Debt has ruined many marriages after the honeymoon. Couples should build their relationship on a solid foundation that will keep them happy together.

Trying to keep up with the expectations from relatives, friends, and the crowd can ruin a love relationship.

A reality check is important concerning finances and what kind of marriage ceremony the couple can afford, as well as where they can afford to live. Simplicity in budgeting finances is key to financial management.

Spiritual Dimension of Love

IT IS WORTH noting that couples ought to seek spiritual guidance before committing to live with each other. Love and marriage is a spiritual undertaking. Marriage is between two people but the union affects family members and future offspring. Serious thought needs to be taken before one gets married. Some decisions should be made before a crisis comes and basic principles like faith in God, religious affiliation, number of children the couple plan to have, financial decisions, handling relatives, and deciding where to live should be settled well beforehand.

Romantic love involves strong emotions. Emotions are developed as you spend time together and exchange kind words and acts with each other. The more time you spend getting to know each other, the more you bond with each other. It becomes very difficult to break the bond if realizing the relationship has to end.

When a couple believes in the permanence of marriage, they will seek the true foundation of love. God knows how we can get the best and the most out of our relationships because He is the Author of Love. Adhering to the love principles as outlined in the Word of God can help couples prevent and overcome the heartache of breakups and divorce. (1 Corinthians 13: 4-7)

The Romantic Dimension

Humans are spiritual beings by nature. Everyone worships someone or something. Every human being has a spirit. Being spiritual means you have a belief system that governs your way of life. Falling in love is a spiritual undertaking. You connect with someone you romantically love in a spiritual sense. Let us look at how you feel and behave when you fall in love.

You think of that person all the time.

When you see the person you love, you feel "butterflies in your stomach."

You have the desire to be with them all the time.

Time flies faster when you are together and you do not seem to have enough time together.

You have the desire to give them the best gifts you can afford.

You adore their looks and feel they are the most handsome/beautiful person in the world.

You want them to have the best in life.

You want everyone close to you to know them.

You want to protect them from any harm. You'd rather sacrifice your life to save their life in times of danger. In other words, you focus your attention on this particular individual in a special way that is so different than how you relate to others in general.

Romantic love is a spiritual encounter. It changes your life forever in many ways. Even when the relationship comes to an end, in one way or another, the effects of love on each other remain with the lovers a long time.

Romantic love is spiritual because it is a mystery. No one can explain the experience. It is a spiritual encounter. All those who fall in love admit that they cannot explain how it happened. It is so supernatural and surreal. That is why before one falls completely in love, basic fundamentals ought to be agreeable to both.

Romantic Influence On Human Life

ROMANTIC LOVE IS the most beautiful relationship that a human being can ever experience with another human being on planet earth.

It is the most powerful and overwhelming state of being that can involve two people.

Romantic love is the sacred relationship between a man and a woman.

It is the power that drives men and women to do great wonderful things in the name of love, and it is the motivating factor behind accomplishments and ambitions for the sake of the beloved.

Falling in love cannot be described It must be experienced.

Falling in love is not an end but a means to directly love the Creator. It opens a new horizon and lenses through which you begin to look at the world.

New songs about romantic love are composed every day. New movies and dramas about romance are made every day. We seem to never get enough of romantic love.

The Romantic dimension

Romantic love is an inspiration for many artists. Many books are written about romance; be it fiction or autobiography, there is often an element of love. Betrayed love, jilted love, unrequited love, or true love experienced are all topics that are written about.

Romantic love touches our lives a thousand ways, directly or indirectly.

People fall in love in times of war and in times of peace.

Even during wartime, people have managed to fall in love with the person their country considers an enemy. Romantic love is an amazing love.

When couples ignore romantic love, their marriage takes a different turn. Eventually they begin to treat each other as strangers. Then the idea of love completely disappears and they lose each other in the business of paying bills, working long hours, raising kids, etc. Romantic love cannot be ignored without negative emotional or even marital consequences.

Nature of Love

*L*OVE IS THE greatest asset humans can count on.

Love is irreplaceable, undefeated, and resilient.

Love is a safety net to relationships, families, workplaces, and communities at large.

Many things you do without love will harm you or others in the long run.

Love is the thread that holds the fabric of humanity together.

Love is powerful. The power of love is manifested at all times when hate and indifference threaten to exterminate human life. Love has always conquered hate in all its forms.

Love overpowers and conquers all types of discrimination towards races, tribes, genders, and socio-economic classes of people. Love has historically defeated slavery and genocide. The world cannot exist without love.

Love affects every fabric of our lives no matter who you are or where you live. An attempt to ignore love and to trample on it is to shake the foundation of your well-being and others around you.

Love should be the foundation of what you do and how you treat other humans on this planet. When love is not the motivating factor

The Romantic dimension

in your dealings, your heart becomes empty, vain, and eventually dangerous.

Love is the fabric of the network that holds and connects humans to each other from the beginning of creation.

When you begin to love, you begin to live and become productive. Many inventions in technology were discovered when someone was determined to find a solution to a problem affecting humanity.

Ignoring love is ignoring yourself. Your body functions well when you love and receive love from others. Allowing yourself to love and to be loved, is a sure way to heal past scars and pain in the heart.

Everyone will experience love or rejection at one point or another in many ways in this life. When you face rejection, you have a choice to believe you can still experience love another time.

Lack of love kills millions every day. Decisions made without consideration for the well-being of people, impact the masses. Going to war, raising taxes, withholding food stamps, raising tuition, selling contaminated food items, or using dangerous chemicals in drugs and manufactured goods are all acts that can adversely impact other humans. When love for humanity comes before profits, lives will be saved. Therefore, love cannot be confined to a relationship alone.

External forces can impact marital relationships positively or negatively.

Some of the decisions made at board rooms or in work places can negatively or positively affect individual marital relationships.

Broken marriages affect millions of children all over the world. Every child wishes their parents would love each other for their safety net.

Broken marriages can create negative impact on an individual financial wellbeing.

Broken marriage can affect family members and a community negatively.

Broken marriages can impact negatively on government ability to provide social and economic wellbeing to its citizens.

Many young teenagers who come from broken relationships perceive that their parents did not love them enough to stay together. Some will harbor rebellion against teachers, parents, government authority, and even God.

Love will not seek its own pleasure at the expense of other's pain. Before a break up where children are involved, couples need to seek professional counselling, forgiveness, and change of behaviors and lifestyles that hurt and break families. Divorce is painful. It is like a death to families, but forgiveness and repentance of wrongs done to each other can heal the couple when both are willing to change something about their doomed relationship.

Love will always beg you to see it, touch it, feel it, and embrace it. Love appears in unexpected places and circumstances.

Love can appear in a child's smile, from a pet, from a stranger, and even from an enemy. Never ignore love just because it has come from a strange, unexpected source. Love will always surprise you.

Love cannot be ignored, no matter how blind you are to it. Love appears and shines like the new day sun even when you are not searching for it.

Love brightens lives and heals the broken hearted.

Each time you compromise love you set a stage for failure. Burying love is promoting mediocrity in all areas of life. When you settle for mediocre relationships, your heart will still long for the real thing. You will always feel empty and void in your heart until you allow love to permeate your relationships and your ambitions.

To be in love, one has to learn to be vulnerable. Exposing your true self to someone is very scary to some people. This kind of fear prevents one from fully loving and becoming loveable. Love can overcome fear.

The Romantic dimension

Everyone longs for love. Every heart longs to connect to deep feelings, cares, concerns, and happiness with someone. We just need to learn to know what it takes to love someone and be lovable.

Love operates on the following principles:

Love cannot be imposed or forced on anyone. No matter how much you love someone, if they do not love you back the circle of that love is not complete. There cannot be a healthy relationship where love is one-sided.

Love cannot be coerced. Loving enough to let go is a noble principle.

True love must be legitimate. When you claim to love someone, you must respect their relationships with other people before you met them. It is selfish to expect someone to leave their spouse or lover for you. You need to respect other people's relationships no matter how attracted you feel towards them. It is wise to avoid the disaster of love triangles. Dating a married man in hopes that he will divorce his wife and come to you is a sure way to start a doomed relationship from the beginning.

True love waits. Human hearts are not mechanical machines which perform automatically. Hearts cannot be programmed to love at any time and break up and love again without scars. Love cannot and should not be rushed. Love must be given time to take roots, then be cultivated, and mature into a full blown relationship before you go to the next level. One should not skip the stages of falling in love.

Love does not ignore compatibility. 'Birds of the same feather flock together.' Cultivate what you have in common with the person you are trying to love. Avoid extreme gaps in age, education, and sometimes be careful about compromising certain cultural and religious values. Recognize the stumbling blocks or pitfalls ahead of time so that both can make decisions to proceed or cut short the relationship.

Genuine love, loves the individual, not their title, fame, bank account, belief system, race, or tribe. A human being is whole without the trappings of power, money, influence, or ethnicity.

Loving someone means fulfilling their needs, before you address your own needs and wants.

Envying what others have is not love. Admiring someone can turn into love when you take time to know them for who they are and not what they do or what their bank account looks like.

Romantic love is a spiritual undertaking. When you love someone, you meet their spiritual needs. It means doing what is best for the one you love. It can also mean not being in a relationship with them if it is not in their best interest. That is true love.

When you meet someone who is wealthy, your focus should be how you can enrich their lives in other ways not on how you can benefit from their wealth. When you meet a pretty face, your goal should be how you will pour your love into her to make her life joyful and to help her fulfill her dreams, not on how you can exploit their beauty and treat them like an acquired trophy. In the long run, when real intention is not about the person but what they have, or their influence, disappointment is inevitable.

When your focus on an individual is based on their wealth, beauty, or fame, then you lose the true value of the individual. The value of a human cannot be measured by their looks, possessions, or fame. Humans are created in the image of God. Everyone needs to be loved as a whole person with or without the trappings of power, fame, or wealth.

Jesus values human life and that is why He sacrificed His own life to save ours. Therefore, the value of a human is the life of Christ. Once you value an individual in the light of the priceless value that God has placed on them, you no longer demand to be loved, but take the first step to love. (Ephesians 5: 2, 21)

When your interest in someone is about their possessions and beauty or fame it means you only love yourself, and use others to get what they have. When a relationship is based on what you gain from

The Romantic dimension

it, failure and pain are inevitable. Love does not take away but gives and receives.

When you love someone, you give them your heart, adoration, devotion, praise, admiration, money, and body. You give them yourself. You cannot love without giving.

Love is what you give to the beloved without expecting anything in return. It is making someone happy at your own loss. That is supreme love. Those who love find life.

Love has been constant through the ages. It has maintained the same principles since the beginning of life. It has appeared and has been recorded in human history among all nations, races, tribes and languages. Love still exits and millions of people are still searching for love. Whoever finds love finds life.

Love stories are endless. Every day people are still writing their individual love stories. Here are some of the past love stories people are familiar with;

Love appeared the day Eve brought the forbidden fruit to her husband Adam, who ate the fruit knowing they would die from the consequence of eating the Fruit of God. I believe Adam could not imagine life without Eve and betrayed God for her. Actually, Adam committed spiritual suicide that day for the woman he loved. 1 Timothy 2; 14

Abraham married Hagar to please his wife Sarah and threw Hagar into the wilderness when Sarah wanted her out. Isaac loved Rebecca at first sight. Jacob loved Rachel and her kids among other wives. For the love of her late husband, Ruth could not let go of her mother in-law Naomi and moved from her country to care for Naomi. Solomon loved the Shulamite shepherd woman he met in the field and wrote the Song of Solomon from the romantic experience he had with her. The Taj Mahal temple was built in honor of a loved woman by her husband.

Marriage and family is an opportunity that is given to exercise love. Those who do not love their family members cannot and will not love others out there in the political world, in religious positions, or celebrities. The more power an unloving person has, the more people he will hurt on his trail. We read this all the time in the media. Therefore, the most dangerous person is one who does not know love.

Interpersonal Relationships

It is important to recognize that men and women are different in their perception of romantic love. It is crucial to understand that the needs of your spouse are different from your own.

Needs A Man In Marrieage

A MAN DOES NOT want sex, he needs it. When a wife denies sex to her husband, the husband feels rejected, and that rejection affects his male psychology in many other ways. Sexual fulfilment is a priority need for a man in marriage.

A man needs honor from his wife. It means a lot to a man when his wife has a good reputation among family members and in society.

To a man honor is respecting his views, his work, and recognizing his achievements. Respecting his parents and especially his mother. A man needs a woman he can trust with his secrets and personal issues without fearing betrayal.

A man feel respected when his wife behaves and speaks to him with dignity in public.

A man needs to feel he is appreciated by the woman he loves and to know that he is her hero. A man needs a woman who needs him and acts like he is doing something to make her life better. When a man feels he has nothing to do for a woman, he feels like a failure. This is why a well-adjusted man works hard to care for his family. When that role is taken over by his woman or someone else, he can feel unaccomplished.

The Romantic dimension

A man needs a woman who will say to him in words and actions that she is loyal to him, especially when the world is hostile and in times of failure, economic difficulties, or defeat of any kind.

A man is not naturally wired to think domestically, however, he can perform domestic work by learning or according to how he was raised. A man thinks of other things like houses, cars, land, sports, and business. In other words, men see things from above while women see things from below. This means the woman has a better vision when it comes to domestic affairs. A woman by her nature has a better sense of domestic priorities over a man. Therefore, a woman should learn domestic management as one of the ways to meet a man's needs and for family stability.

No man wants to be compared to other men. A man feels a sense of uniqueness when treated as an accomplished individual even if it means being appreciated for little things like paying bills, cleaning the yard, washing dishes, and coming home for dinner on time. To a man, this is respect and honor. This is love.

No man would like to spend time with and live with a nagging woman. Nagging someone to constantly do your will is immoral coercion. A man wishes to live in a peaceful environment with the woman he loves. (Proverbs 9:13)

A man needs a woman who can clean the house and cook. These skills help a man to want to come home to relax and to eat home cooked meals and be around his wife.

A man needs a woman who opens her mouth to speak with wisdom and politeness. In other words, a woman should develop the art of proper communication skills to make her husband listen to her.

A man needs a woman who is well-informed about social –political issues and sometimes the sports world so that he can have a conversation with her in his field of interest.

A man needs a woman who worships God. This means the woman can relate to Divine power to overcome her own demons and to be able to trust her family in the hands of a powerful Being. When a woman has no connection with God, the family has no spiritual foundation because her influence on family is greater than the man's influence.

A man loves a woman who is frugal with her expenditure of their resources.

What Women Expect in Marriage

A WOMAN NEEDS LOVE and affection. It is not a luxury. It is an emotional, psychological, and physical need for a woman to receive love expressed in words and actions. (Ephesians 5.25)

A woman needs financial security. Adam had the world at Creation in Eden and when Eve came into the world, her husband had the world to share with her. To this day, a woman suffers insecurity when there is lack of financial support. The world has changed and resources can be hard to secure. We do not live in an ideal world, but the principle need of a woman, for at the very least the basic material things, has not changed. A woman with virtue, however, will see beyond the material world.

A woman needs emotional security. Violence against women by men is very common in all communities of the world. Women suffer abuse of all kinds in their marriages. A good man will protect his woman from his unkindness, infidelity, and all manners of unfaithfulness. The wife needs to believe she can completely trust her husband with her life.

The Romantic dimension

A woman needs a man who can help with the day-to-day running of the household such as helping kids with homework, tucking kids into bed, helping with showers, and general household chores. Due to modern-day financial needs, many women work outside of the home while raising kids. A wise husband will see it fit to help the family stay put by making sure the wife is not overworked.

A woman needs a husband who meets her sexual needs. A lot of emphasis is put on male needs for sexual fulfilment in magazines and books and on how a woman should sexually make sure her man is happy. A woman's sexual fulfilment promotes her mental and spiritual well-being. Most women do not reach orgasm during sexual intimacy, which is bad for the relationship and for her happiness. Both partners need to talk about sexuality to make sure the woman has orgasms so she can be happy and sexually fulfilled.

A woman needs a man who respects her femininity. Women are different from men biologically. A wise man will study to adopt and support his woman as she goes through the changes at all stages of life. From the day a woman gets her period to the day she has sex, becomes a wife, gets pregnant, becomes a mother, and eventually goes through menopause, she will not be the same person you married. These changes affect women in more drastic ways than men can keep up with. However, being aware of these changes can prepare a man to deal with the crisis at every stage of her life.

A woman needs a man who is not afraid to express his affection in public.

A woman needs a man who is generous with his money.

A woman needs a man who works hard to financially support her and their family.

A woman needs a man who can protect her against hostile members of his family and her critics. A husband should not wring his hands and do nothing when his side of the family are constantly talking ill of his wife or treat her unfairly.

What Women Expect In Marriage

A woman needs a man who supports her career ambitions even when her income is bigger than his or she is more famous than him. In other words, a man who is not threatened by her achievements and success.

Understanding the needs of each other and fulfilling those needs within your ability is key to successful marriage.

Every couple have their own unique circumstances and dynamics. The bottom line is to make sure the couple is happy in their union.

How Romantic Love Flows

WHEN YOU LOVE someone, you express that love with admiration. You admire their looks, laughter, voice, mannerisms, how they walk and talk, etc. You admire their eyes, legs, hair, hands, feet, and color. You begin to appreciate their unique personality and appearance. It is the art of loving the person in their beauty and imperfections.

Romantic love must be expressed in action and must be received by the object of your love to complete the circle of love. When love is not received, it becomes void. Love is complete and fulfilled when it is received and appreciated by the beloved.

Romantic love must be expressed in words and actions. Love that is not expressed, does not exist.

You should not assume someone loves you, if they do not tell you and do not deliberately show it by their actions.

Romantic love is exclusive. It can only involve two people. It is impossible to love two people at the same time. Maintaining a love life means being faithful to yourself, your spouse, and your Creator God.

Romantic love needs spiritual and cultural compatibility as a bedrock foundation.

The Romantic dimension

Romantic love involves sensual feelings and strong emotions. Therefore, you must handle each other with care. You must say what you mean and mean what you say. Assurance of your devotion and love should be genuine and constant.

Romantic love must be cultivated by spending quality and quantity time together.

Stumbling blocks to love flow

IGNORANCE IS ONE of the enemies of progress in all aspects of life. You cannot give what you do not possess. Therefore, you must learn the meaning of love and the difference between romantic love and other love connections like loving your parents, siblings, friends, and everyone else. Taking time to study romantic love and its pitfalls is wisdom. Millions of people believe love just happens like a mosquito bite. It just happens to you and you have no control over whom you love. While at times it might feel that way, the truth is that when that same person does something that hurts you, then you suddenly change your mind about them and even walk away from the relationship. This is proof that while you can get emotionally attracted to someone, it is a choice you make to be in the relationship. Love involves choices. Ignorance about love is very costly. It costs you happiness in this life and ultimately eternal life.

Shortsightedness is refusing to see beyond what you know and believe. In order to get the most and the best out of a relationship you must discard myths and superstitions about love and marriage. Take time to learn what make relationships work and what makes them fail. Knowledge is power.

The Romantic dimension

Neglecting to create time to be with family; today, we live in hectic lifestyle conditions, and in the process, many couples spend most of their time making money to pay for bills and other things they need and want. Couples sacrifice time with each other and with family to work overtime to get extra cash. Divorce and separation result from a lack of putting family first over all other things. Balance between work and family time is crucial in today's economy. You reap what you sow.

Carelessness entering into marital relationships with people you hardly know can hurt you; before you fall in love, try to know the person's background, work history, family, beliefs, morality, and how they spend their time and money. Remember, a branch does not fall far from the tree. There are patterns and behaviors that are common in families. Once you establish that the person's background can accommodate yours, then you can proceed to venture into the relationship and commit to it. This process hardly ever happens these days. Many people meet, a few days later have sex, and then try to know who it is they are sleeping with. When you have high esteem for yourself, you will not carelessly throw yourself at a stranger only to deal with the consequences later.

1. Before marriage, you need to date someone who has the same values as you have. If you believe in health and temperance, you should know how to cook healthy meals, dress well, maintain clean living conditions, respect people, and have decent conversations without using cursing or foul language. Before you marry someone you must establish their manners when disagreements occur. Couples who misbehave during disagreements cannot handle relationships. Everyone needs marital counseling before getting married.

2. Refusing to learn is actually Stubbornness which can impede your marital bliss. This is one of the evils that retards the

growth of a relationship. Stubbornness blinds its own victim to an extent that they do not see what others see in them. It is a form of pride and ignorance. No one is right all the time, and if you maintain a constant sense of self-righteousness, you will be alone the rest of your life. Those who are stubborn will not enjoy the beauty of love as they create controversies and disagreements every step of the way. When there is stubbornness, love will always be choked by arguments and fights.

3. Monotony can make what is beautiful look ugly. Make an effort to go out and discover new ways to express love. Go out and enjoy beautiful nature. Travel if you can, and experience different foods and cultures. Don't allow yourself to get stuck in the past or fixated on the future. Seize moments and take pictures of those good moments for good memories. Put color in your love life. Read good books on interesting issues. Love life and discard fear of the unknown. Get out of your comfort zone and wear new hairstyles, dresses, and make changes in your diet. Decide to surprise your spouse. Do everything within your power to avoid monotony.

4. A passive attitude is in fact a form of laziness. Romantic love must be passionate, deliberate, and full of enthusiasm. When one is passive in a love relationship, boredom and staleness become inevitable.

An Epic Love Story

In Genesis 29-33 we read the love story of Jacob and Rachel. Jacob met Rachel at the well. He fell in love at first sight. He was overjoyed when he kissed her for the first time and could not help himself but wailed in ecstasy, and for 7 years he worked to raise enough bridal dowry to marry his beloved.

I imagine this couple meeting in secret to exchange their feelings for each other, holding hands, kissing, looking at the sunset, exchanging gifts, and hugging each other tightly before parting from their meeting place. I picture them gazing deeply into each other's eyes before saying good night. For seven years, love bloomed and matured. The laughter, the kisses, the holding of hands, and the warm embrace were not all coming to an end but to the climax when the romantic emotional tension was to be relieved in consummation of their marriage. The waiting was over when the wedding day was announced. At long last Jacob and Rachel could love and live together forever in holy matrimony. After the wedding, Jacob woke up to a rude shock of his life. His bride was another woman, not Rachel.

In order to marry Rachel, the woman he loved, Jacob worked for her father Laban who kept reducing Jacob's wages as the years went by. But his love for Rachel was greater than the toil he endured under the

The Romantic dimension

cruel Laban. To crown his cruelty to Jacob, Laban and his daughter Leah conspired to rob Jacob of the most precious moment he had waited and worked for, for seven years. On the wedding night, Leah was on his bed. In the morning, he could not believe the sight. Rachel was not the bride but Leah. Jacob got out of the bed and ran out to look for his beloved Rachel. But before he could find Rachel he met Laban.

According to Laban's traditional belief, his first-born daughter Leah had to get married first before he could marry off Rachel. He sacrificed the happiness of his daughters on the Altar of Tradition. With one blow, Laban made her daughters hate each other and caused Jacob to become a polygamist. Made Leah the hated wife, and Rachel became the jealous wife. The history of Jacob took a negative twist in one night. His children with Leah hated Rachel's children.

Jacob's Love For Rachel

FOR THE SEVEN years that Jacob spent loving Rachel, he completely immersed himself in working hard under tough conditions in order to marry the first and the last and the *only* woman he ever loved.

The morning after the wedding night, when he realized he was given the wrong woman, he still went out to get Rachel. Laban the money lover set another price to get Rachel. Jacob had to work another seven years to get married to Rachel.

Laban, like a Red eyed Dragon, had watched Jacob's love for Rachel grow more and more each day and each year and was waiting to strike him with the most cruel lie and deceit of a millennium. While Jacob loved Laban's daughter Rachel, Laban laid in wait to strike Jacob like a poisonous snake that strikes unsuspecting victim. Laban succeeded in his scheme but he lost the love and eventually the presence of his daughters, just as Jacob never saw his mother Rebecca who 20 years back had convinced him to swindle his own brother Esau of his birthright. It is very important to study the characters of a family tree.

When Jacob had enough of Laban's schemes, he decided to leave secretly to go back to his homeland. Laban followed Jacob in order to harm him, but God appeared to him and warned him not to

The Romantic dimension

harm Jacob. However, Rachel had hidden Laban's gods, and after his searching and harassing of Jacob's family, Jacob swore to the God of heaven. By the time Laban left and kissed his daughters good bye he had left a curse through Jacob against Rachel. And Rachel died during childbirth to her second born Benjamin.

Jacob still loved Rachel even in death. He turned his attention to Rachel's two sons Joseph and Benjamin. Leah and her children and the maids' children could not be loved as much as Jacob loved Joseph and Benjamin. On his deathbed, Joseph had the most blessings, and Joseph's two sons' names were included in the composition of the twelve tribes of the Israelites by dropping off the list the names of the other brothers of Joseph.

The story of Jacob and Rachel is an illustration of how romantic love operates. Time spent together loving each other cannot be erased by a sexual encounter with others. Jacob, a virgin man, had sex for the first time with someone he did not love. Upon realization of the truth in the morning, he did not love Leah simply because he had sex with her. Sex can never replace love. Leah kept having children with the man who despised her every day of his life.

Jacob, Rachel, Leah and their children

While the Bible records polygamy among God's servants, it also records the results and the consequences of those choices. Jacob, his wives, his concubines, and his children's story are written as a lesson to the readers of the Holy Book. We learn the betrayals, murderer's plots, pain, forgiveness, and restoration.

Through the forgiveness from Joseph, Jacob's family was able to unite and move on from the sin of betrayals. We can only heal from the pain of betrayals when embrace to forgive those who have hurt us.

Marriages of convenience

TODAY, VERY FEW communities arrange marriages for their sons or daughters, but still some people would willingly choose to enter into marriages of convenience. Most of these types of relationships include but are not limited to:

a. Financial gain
b. Sexual exploitation
c. Job promotion
d. Pregnancy out of wedlock
e. Poverty
f. Religious reasons
g. Traditional reasons
h. Racial or tribal reasons

Anytime, anywhere, and in any situation, marriages or relationships of convenience will hurt those involved. **It is hard to be** happy when you marry someone you do not love or one who does not love you.

1. When couples realize, for whatever reason, they entered into a marriage of convenience, they both can begin to work on how

they can learn to love one another. It might be difficult, but it is possible.

Marriages based on financial gain

This type of marriage of convenience is the most common type.

People want to be financially stable, and money provides comfort and luxury. People with extra money can have influence in politics, fame, and celebrity syndrome. Money makes one to be envied by their neighbors, friends, and relatives. The more money you have, the more influential you might be in politics, in your community, in the work place, and in religious circles. Having money brings the illusion of being successful, even if you stole the money or earned it illegally, a lot of people will still envy you. Often women who do not value themselves will flock around men with money and power despite their age, morality, or abuse record. Often men with power and money will go for the women with pretty looks. It sounds like money can get a pretty face. Any rich, famous, or wealthy man should ask himself whether he is using his wealth and influence to get a spouse. And if that is the case, how sure are you that the person is in love with you and not your money. Money is good and everyone needs money, however, money cannot buy happiness, peace of mind, and love. Money can buy attention, but cannot change a heart.

Relationships based on sexual exploitation

Sexual attraction is important in all marital relationships. However, sexual attractions cannot be an end in and of itself. When it is, then it means an exploitation. Physical intimacy should be a result of a developed relationship.

Sexual exploitation occurs when individuals use sex to get something from each other or when one individual takes advantage of a minor person in age, a person with a disability, a poor person, or an employee.

Sexual exploitation can also be used as a trap to get favors, promotions, and even as a scheme to compromise and bring down a prominent individual in society from a powerful position.

Selfish individuals use sex as a weapon to get their way or to harm others.

Love should be the only reason to have sex.

Both partners should be in love with each other to consent to sexual intercourse. When the idea of love is used as bait to be intimate, it is still an exploitation.

Since men need sex and women need love, both men and women can mask their intentions and exploit each other.

Evil women have historically used sex to trap men and to cause them to fall from power like in the case of Samson and Delilah, in Judges 13.

David used his power to commit adultery with Bathsheba in 2 Samuel 11:2-6.

His sexual misconduct accounts in the Bible are meant for our education and are not meant to shame the Men of God. They were good people who made wrong decisions. We are urged by these stories to care for others first before our wants and needs.

The only reason to get married to someone should be because you love that person and you cannot live without them. That person should be the one with whom you want to share good moments and bad moments. The one whose perfections and imperfections are acceptable to you. The one you love even when they are annoying. Yes, the one you admire, you respect, and you adore. The one you will do anything for in order to make their lives joyful. The one you want to protect from all harm. The one you can still love even when they wrong you. Yes, the one you love how they walk, talk, look, sleep, laugh, sing,

The Romantic Dimension

and play. You have to love the whole person in order for your love to be genuine.

This type of love can be developed with time spent together in cultivating the relationship. This is why loving someone from the heart cannot be determined by religion, traditions, or race. Religion, traditions, and race are important elements that shape a person's morality, upbringing, and identity. But, the three elements do not determine a person's ability to love. A happy marriage is developed by love, discipline, morality, knowledge, and determination from both partners.

A happy marriage where husband and wife are happy with each other is the only way to protect the children in that relationship. When the marriage is bad, the children are hurt. So parents who love their children must love each other by forgiving ills done to each other to protect their children from their selfishness.

The Triumph of Love

No one can claim victory when there are no battles to be won. Love must be tried, tested, and shaken in order to remain firm and resilient.

Some of the most common challenges couples will face over the period of their love life are:

1. Trust: those who love and marry each other have some degrees or level of trust. Trust is earned.

2. You trust people who have shown caring gestures and keep their promises.

3. Couples can lose trust when one of both are not dependable. While transparency and honesty should be paramount in a relationship, individuality must be respected and honored.

4. You trust those who can sacrifice time and money for you.

The Romantic dimension

5. You trust the one who empathizes with your sorrows and disappointments. And the one who never joins the crowd to condemn you when you are wrong and have failed.

6. You trust the person who allows you to be vulnerable around them without taking advantage of the situation.

7. You trust the person who forgives you when they have reason not to

8. You trust the person who loves you in spite of your imperfections and accept you as you are.

9. You trust the one who does not get inconvenienced with your flaws.

In a nut shell, you trust the one who loves you in spite of your weaknesses.

Love cannot thrive where trust has been buried.

Faithfulness is a virtue that few people have today. Life is full of temptations that beg you left and right not to remain true to your spiritual beliefs and moral upbringing. Unfaithfulness in financial and moral matters affects marital relationships all the time, in all places, and in all stages of life.

Faithfulness to your spouse is a protection shell around your relationship. Love needs the foundation of faith.

Your love will be tried in so many ways checking your will to remain true. When you fail once, you cannot afford to stay in that place. You need to get up and start afresh. The fight to protect your love should be endless.

The Holiness Of Sex

SEX IS HOLY. Holy means set apart. Sex is beautiful and those who have never had sex are always curious as to what it feels like to have sex. Sexual intercourse is an encounter of a spiritual kind. The first person you will have sex with is very important. Sexual intercourse changes our lives completely, positively or negatively depending on with whom how, where, and why you have sex

We go to churches, synagogues, mosques, and family altars to declare our love and commitment to each other during marriage ceremonies or weddings because we want our romantic life to be acknowledged and blessed by God and humanity. Sex is an expression of a committed love. You declare your stand to the whole world that you only love the individual before God and before men and that the only person you want to love sexually is that one person

You need certain qualifications to have sex. They are as follows:

a. You should be of legal age to have sex and be mature enough to be able to handle sexual activity with a fully grown partner.

b. Both partners should be ready spiritually, emotionally, and should be economically independent.

The Romantic Dimension

    c. You must be in a committed marriage relationship to engage in holy sexual intercourse. When intimacy is preferred over commitment, you will definitely run into situations where one or both will be hurt. Sex without love is sinful because physical intimacy is an expression of love in the heart.

    d. Lust can be confused with love but they have opposite meanings.

Unplanned sexual intercourse is dangerous. Physical intimacy is a special event that should not happen impulsively with strangers, relatives, the boss in his office, employees, neighbors, the mailman, etc. Such acts are an indication of low self-worth and lack of moral sense. If you can plan other things in your life, planning to have good fulfilling love-based sexual intercourse, only in marriage is wisdom. Random sex is dangerous and can lead to either disease, unwanted pregnancy, or death.

    e. You must be ordained into a committed relationship to be legally binding to your spouse. Since sex is holy, you need to be ordained to have sex.

    f. Presidents of countries all over the world are sworn in before they ascend to power. Kings and queens have to be crowned before ascending to their thrones. Gospel ministers must be ordained to serve their congregations. One should be ordained into marriage vows before sexual intercourse. This is to make both partners have the right to intimacy with each other following their vows. This ordination is meant to keep husband and wife committed to each other and to honor their Creator and to honor their families and their communities. This commitment would ensure children are secured in this relationship.

g. Casual sexual intercourse with someone who is no one to you is a way to kill the principle of love from your heart. No one can satisfy lust, just like no one can satisfy gluttony. You must learn the meaning of loving another human being before you engage in sexual activity. And when you embrace love for another person in your heart, then you think about what is for the best interest of the other person, not your interest. You must consider whether you love them and whether they equally love you. It takes time to figure this out. But when you get involved in sexuality before you figure out about love, you will likely run into problems. When you ignore the rules of love and sexuality, pain, suffering, and disappointment is inevitable. This is why you must recognize that sex is holy and each time we mess with the holy things of God, we tend to mess up our own lives.

h. Love for your spouse expressed in sexual intercourse is the only way to satisfy your desire for sexual fulfilment. Sex becomes the means to fulfill love and not the other way around.

i. Sex should fulfill the desire for love and cause the heart to feel wholesome with satisfaction.

j. When one accepts to be ordained into holy matrimony, they accept the terms of God about marriage and family and they say to God in front of the crowd that they will abide by God's standard of love until they die. By doing this, they also call upon the powers of God to secure their love for each other and to protect their marriage.

The Romantic dimension

k. There are no illegitimate children in this world. However, there is illegitimate sex that produces children with non-committed lovers.

l. Whether one believes in God's standard of love and sexuality or not, the results of illicit sex affect everyone involved in it negatively either in the present or in the future. The natural laws of relationships apply to all humans regardless of their belief system.

m. God's standard of love and sex is one husband and one wife. Sexual intercourse in a private place to honor their bodies and each other and to protect their dignity in the society. Which means sex with the right person at the right time and the right place. Order is Divine. Intimate sexual moments should be private as the act of sex is unity of emotional rhythm and a spiritual and physical connection that involves the whole personality of an individual. When we recognize the depth of sexuality and value our sexuality with utmost care.

n. When God created you, He created your brain to think, your eyes to see, your nose to smell, your mouth to eat and speak, your ears to hear, your hands to work, your legs to walk, and your private parts for sex and procreation. Every part of your body has a function that the Creator put into place and in an orderly fashion. One part of your body can only perform its function. There is also order in nature: the sun will not perform the function of the moon, the bird will not act like a snake or the flower to perform the function of a tree. Only humans try to willfully interfere with the natural laws of the Creator.

o. Each time one breaks the moral laws of nature, there is a consequence that affects every fabric of society. Each time sexual immorality takes place, people get hurt immediately or later. For example, when one becomes involved in unsafe or illicit sex, most of the time in secret, unwanted pregnancy or sexually transmitted disease could be the result. The woman might choose to abort the baby, in this case the baby dies for her wrong choices. If she keeps the baby, she might become a single mother if the other partner does not want to be involved with the baby. Sometimes the woman aborts or keeps the baby against the sexual partner's wishes or even knowledge. And in cases of sexually transmitted disease, future partners could be infected too. These painful and unwanted consequences happen in cases when people have multiple sexual partners, and relationships with no agreements of commitments. The point is, each time we break the natural laws of love, sex, and family, we all get hurt or hurt other people. A wise man will care about the woman's wellbeing before they both engage in sexual activity. More women than men become single parents due to broken or illicit relationships.

p. The natural law of marriage is: fall in love, take time to know and accept the person fully, commit yourself to the person forever, marry the person, and have sex forever only with that person.

q. The world does not offer ideal situations. Relationships might be interrupted by separation, divorce, or death of a loved one. It is unfortunate that we live in this kind of a world, but even though this is so, one should make wise decisions when life gives them one or several chances to do so.

The Romantic dimension

r. Sex is very important to God and to humanity. If there were no sex, there would be no humans born in this world. God created sex for enjoyment and for procreation. But when we abuse or misplace our sexual activities, the sequence of order is broken and we get hurt by breaking the rules that safeguard our sexuality. Sex in marriage relationship is a safe way to avoid the pain associated with marital cheating and infidelity that plagues many relationships today.

s. Sexual intercourse involves sharing strong emotional attachments, mental attachments, spiritual connections, physical attachments and the exchange of DNA with each other. The process of conception during sexual intercourse is a mystery. If there is one part of your life you need to pay attention to the most, it is in choosing your marital sexual partner.

t. The children born out of a sexual union reflect the physical traits and genetic characteristics from both parents. The offspring are created in both the man's and the woman's image. Just like the Creator proclaimed in the beginning, "Let us create man in our image and likeness." The process to bring another human being into the world should not be taken lightly. It is the Creator's plan to populate the earth, and therefore He is concerned with our well-being in all matters and that includes our sexual well-being

Your actions touch the lives of other human beings God created through human sexuality. Those human beings include the children you bring into this world; they are His before they are yours. Their safety and happiness is His plan for them and for you. That is why marriage, sex, and children are His business. When we allow His

Divine love to rule our hearts, we can truly love and protect our loved ones with affection and care.

    v.   When one partner ignorantly or knowingly engages in any kind of sexual immorality, they hurt themselves with guilt and confusion. They hurt their partner, children, and God who loves all who are hurting. They also hurt the close members of the family like parents, siblings, and even neighbors and friends.

Sexual intercourse with no commitment not only hurts individuals but also hurts others in the future. A child who grows up not knowing who their Daddy is can be hurt, a woman or a man left to care for a child can be hurt. A grandmother who has to take care of a child who is abandoned may be burdened and the list goes on. Because of God's love for humanity, He gave us his Divine laws to safeguard our relationships.

- While some religious sects and cultures practice polygamy, however, it is not God's ideal marriage arrangements from the beginning of creation. God created one woman (Eve) for one man (Adam). And the life accounts of the biblical patriarchs who practiced polygamy, were filled with betrayals, fights, and in some cases even murder. The Creator wants us to learn from the mistakes of His beloved saints. Wise people learn from other's mistakes, but fools wait to learn from their own mistakes. Polygamy in all its forms is disastrous to a romantic relationship. The husband always loves one woman over the other wives. This leaves the other wives and children to fight over the attention of the man and controversies, competitions, and jealousy leave behind trails of disastrous betrayals and even violence in its path.

The Romantic dimension

Modern-day men in many developed countries do not practice polygamy due to civil laws in their communities, but millions of men still have mistresses. The result of illicit affairs is the same. The legal wives and the children feel betrayed by the man they love. Love betrayed is a lethal weapon for disaster and scandals. Many scandals among prominent personalities in high political positions involve illicit sexual affairs. Therefore, wise prominent people in our society who want to maintain their high positions in society must stay clear of sexual immoralities for their own good and for their families. At the peak of your success, you can become your own enemy and bring yourself down by the choices you make, and fall with a big bang to the benefit of your competitors and enemies.

Sexual misconduct plagues all manner of people in politics, religious organizations, institutions, and communities, therefore no one is safe from sexual misconduct that brings shame and loss of respect and positions. Everyone who wants to be wise must guard their sexual drives for their own security and success.

Why Sexual Security Is Good For Your Well-Being

SEXUAL INTERCOURSE INVOLVES the whole personality: Spiritual mental, emotional, and lastly physical. Sexual intimacy is irrevocable. Once it is done, you cannot take it back by your words.

Sexual intercourse is the ultimate method to express romantic love beyond words. It is an act of total surrender to each other in the deepest spiritual connection between couples. Sex is that serious. This is why rape victims feel something very important and deep was wrongly taken away from them. Rape victims suffer long after the incident. Therefore, sexual intercourse should be voluntary and special to the couple.

Sexual purity means you will avoid having sex with anyone who is not someone to you. Planned sexual union means you have time to sort out your emotions and connection towards your lover and marriage provides that security and is a proof of commitment.

4. Sexual intercourse is the only way you can fully give yourself spiritually, emotionally, mentally, and physically to the other

The Romantic Dimension

person. It is unspoken love. It is love that cannot be expressed in letters. It is the heart speaking with actions of oneness, ecstasy, and intimacy of a spiritual kind. In the moment of this special union, only the two hearts are able to feel the unique giving and receiving of each other in ways only their mind, body, and spirit can express. Sexual intercourse is the most beautiful thing the human heart, body, and mind can enjoy at the same time. This is why what the heart says to the body and to the mind cannot be a lie, it has to speak the truth of its feelings. When sexual intercourse does not have feelings of love for the sexual partner from the heart, then only the body is enjoying the physical union, which means it is not lovemaking. This kind of sexual intercourse is only physical. As one keeps having this kind of sex, the heart is being cheated over and over and the body eventually will stop feeling the urge to have sex as lust takes over love.

Sex is serious business that should never be lightly guarded or regarded. Few people want to have sex with promiscuous individuals. Everyone wants to drink from a clean well, therefore everyone is responsible to keep their well clean.

Each one of us is a product of sexual intercourse between our parents with few exceptions. Which means our parents' choice to be intimate with each other willingly or unwillingly resulted in our being here. That choice impacted our social, economic, racial, genetic, and gender identity. It means our parents' sexual activities have shaped and determined our race, color, genes, geographical environment, and even our personality. Sex is a big deal, do not play with it.

By nature humans need the security of parents for a longer time period than animals. After conception of a baby, it takes nine months for the baby to be born in maturity. It can take 18 to 25 years for a man or woman to be independent from the care of parents financially

Why Sexual Security Is Good For Your Well-being

and emotionally. This is why parents should take responsibility to make sure their children are secure in a loving relationship. All human beings need a loving environment to grow up well-adjusted into adulthood. Each time parents hurt each other they hurt their children. Each time sexual indiscretion takes place in a relationship, the children become victims of the scandals.

Anyone who has ever gone through the process of buying a house, land, or car, knows that the process can be tedious and long. All verifications and scrutiny is tedious. By the time you get your title, you would have to be qualified to get it and whatever you buy would be genuinely scrutinized to make sure the buyer and the seller are both satisfied with the deal. Couples need to think through and go through scrutiny and verifications before venturing into any marital relationship and sexual intercourse in order to be sure you are not getting a shaky relationship.

However, while it is easy to dispose of houses, land and cars, we cannot dispose of human beings so easily. That is why break ups and divorce where children and money are involved always gets ugly and nasty if the couple is not wise. Even in break ups, you need wisdom, fairness, and forgiveness. If you are a victim of a jilted love affair, know that revenge only makes you as bad as your cheating spouse. Each time you seek revenge you lower yourself and your ex will only remember your ugly revenge and not the good person you were before the cheating or betrayal. If you are wise, you will let your goodness haunt them forever. I think that is the best revenge. Jesus said it and I believe it. Turn the other cheek and save yourself the misery of ugly fights over money, children, and properties. I believe if you ever loved someone, you cannot hurt them, because they hurt you. You have to prove that you love to the end. They will not forget that love. Yes, forgiveness is for you to get healing from the hurt. And letting go is noble. Forgiveness is the only way love wins.

The Romantic dimension

You cannot play with fire and escape burning. The wages of sin is death, Romans 6:23. We walk sometimes into our own spiritual pitfalls by the sexual partners we choose, and the love affairs we keep. Illicit sex and misplaced affections can lead to disastrous scandals and hurt many loved ones, yourself, people around you and beyond. Learn to love to avoid sexual misconducts.

How to Get the Best Sex in Marriage

Sexual intercourse is the most beautiful experience humans have in this life. Beautiful love-based sex transforms a personal experience with another human being. Sex makes you feel whole as a woman or as a man. The beauty of sex can only be experienced, not explained.

Mental preparations for sex are very important. This is why couples court and cultivate love and affection, which includes spending quality and quantity time together. Bonding and connection is crucial before sexual intercourse. It means imagining having sex with the person in your mind.

Emotional preparation means falling in love again and again with your lover. Giving your heart fully to the other person. Believing in their love for you and trusting them fully with your whole being. You must allow yourself to be vulnerable to your spouse to be emotionally connected. Discarding all fears and insecurities by addressing issues regarding your relationship.

Physical preparations include holding hands, kissing, watching movies together, sitting on the same chair, gazing into each other's eyes, playing games, and taking a stroll together, hugging tight, and playing with each other. These become memorable moments in time and in the future.

Environmental preparations include a private place to have sex with no distractions like noise, or other people around. Clean bedroom with soft lights. Enough time for foreplay. If preferred, soft

Why Sexual Security Is Good For Your Well-being

instrumental music. The bedroom should be clean and tidy. The air clean and aromatic. The couple should smell good and be patient with each other. Sweet words should be whispered in expression of your admiration for your lover's eyes, cheeks, mouth, hair, and whole body. Assurance of love is very important to a woman before sex and after. The goal is to Make Love.

During sexual intercourse, a man needs to be gentle and caress the woman with his hands and ask the woman when she is ready for penetration. The man should wait until the woman reaches orgasm before ejaculating. Sexual intercourse when the couple is spiritually, emotionally, and mentally connected results in both being able to experience great sex together.

When a couple skips the stages of bonding, their sex life becomes stale and mechanical and that can leave room for sexual malnutrition. It means the body and the heart are longing to be loved both romantically and sexually.

Sexual intercourse is a spiritual undertaking. Couples who want to be sexually fulfilled must strive to meet each other's needs for affection and sexual fulfilment. When couples have a bad sex life, resentment and lack of affection can take over and can affect their marriage. A great sex life depends on love, affection, kindness, gentleness, respect, discipline, and trust. Faith in God helps couples cope during bad times and provides assurance of Divine protection.

Practices that Interfere with Human Sexuality

Pornography is a common sexual intimacy destroyer among many couples who are lured into it by the belief that it is entertainment and might enhance sexual performance. It is a lie that is rarely confronted by many couples. The deeper the individual or couple venture into porn, the lower their sexual taste descends into the bottomless pit. A human being is a whole person, but pornography will turn the mind to obsess on one or some part of the human body and promote sexual lust over relationship. A wholesome sexual relationship is based on loving the whole person and not just part of their body. The human body is the temple of the Holy Spirit and any type of sexual deviation cheapens the sanctity of human life in one way or another. Lust and love do not mean the same thing, just as gluttony and hunger do not mean the same thing.

Female circumcision and genital mutilation are common practices among isolated and primitive tribes in some countries. It is an old, inhumane practice that was meant to slow or eliminate the enjoyment of sexual intercourse by women in those communities. Depending on the seriousness of each mutilation, most of the victims do not have the capability to enjoy sex and some have difficulty during childbirth. Due to their remote dwelling places, few of them have access to give birth through caesarian at a hospital and some die or get serious damage to their genitals after birth which in the end would permanently bar them from ever having sex. Genital mutilation in all its forms is violence against women. Since men from these communities are the ones who enforce these inhumane practices, they should be more educated to understand that they also suffer when their own wives cannot get sexually aroused due to inflicted damage to their genitalia.

Forced marriages happen among certain traditional societies, some religious cults, and among some rich families. Most victims are young women who are forced to marry older men or individuals they have never loved. This fact drastically affects women's sexuality, as it is difficult to enjoy sex with someone you do not love or with whom you have never even had a relationship. Forced marriage is violence against humanity. A wise man would not want to marry a trophy wife who does not love him.

Sex slavery has become common due to poverty, war, and the increase of sexual perversion all over the world. Sex slavery and prostitution affect the natural process of having sex with another human

Why Sexual Security Is Good For Your Well-being

being. Whenever one individual has to sell their body for survival or when they are forced to do it, the sanctity of human life is sacrificed on the altar of lust and exploitation.

Modern-day stress is a sex drive killer. When your mind is taxed with too much work, when you work over eight hours per day, when you are sleepless, and have no time for exercise, your sex life can become unreliable, boring, and stale. We all need a healthy mind and body to have great sexual intercourse. In order to do this, we must maintain a balance between work, rest, and sleep. We must also eat a healthy diet and exercise.

Living conditions and physical appearance can enhance your sexual intimacy or strangle it. "Cleanliness is second to Godliness." You should cultivate living in a clean home. Cluttered living conditions are a sign of carelessness or even mental issues. It means that you are not organized or you might have so many things to do that you fail to live in a clean home environment.

Your appearance is also very crucial to your sex appeal. "Beauty is God given, attractiveness is manmade." You should improve your appearance and love yourself by taking care of your body and your health in general. Remember one of the principles to have great sexual intimacy is to love yourself so that when you are giving yourself to the person you love, you are actually giving what you love. When you love yourself, you give yourself as a gift to your lover which means you give your best.

Sexual attraction includes but is not limited to your way of communication. When you are rude and coarse, you become sexually unattractive. Respect and morality should be maintained even when couples disagree on issues. Using explicit slurs and cursing, demeans your dignity and respect for each other. A gentleman and a lady do not use explicit slurs to belittle one another. Doing this is a sure way to ruin your relationship.

The Romantic dimension

Managing finances: Couples who manage their finances with mutual agreement on expenditures and investments increase sexual intimacy. It is not about how much or little money you have or make but how a couple relates to the management of their income. Both of you must agree on money issues in order to have peace in the marriage. Debts and mismanagement of income brings financial insecurity and therefore, the relationship can be strained. Selfishness and greed should be discarded. Generosity, budgeting, and planning should be practiced by both partners.

Contraceptives and family planning methods can affect sexual intimacy. Some women might not be able to enjoy sexual intimacy when there is fear of an unwanted pregnancy. Some contraceptives reduce sexual desires. Before you get any contraceptives, you need to know all the side effects so you choose what suits your body with the advice of your gynecologist.

Long distance marriage can lead to sexual disaster. While there are circumstances that might force couples to live apart for some time due to some special duty away from home, discipline and morality should be practiced by both partners to protect their relationship.

Diseases or accidental injuries can impede good sexual experience. Life is not predictable. Diseases and accidents can maim one partner. When this occurs, sometimes sexuality is compromised. Love will protect the marriage even when sex fails the couple.

Misguided beliefs about human sexuality can inhibit one from enjoying sex. Some people believe that abstinence from sex equals to holiness. The truth is, abstaining from sexual immorality is holiness. The absence of sex does not equal holiness. Sex is both holy and good. God created a sexual human being with sexual organs to enjoy sex as an expression of love. Being a holy man of God does not cancel your biology.

Drug abuse and alcohol use can affect your sexual performance. Before you indulge in any kind of use of illicit or prescription drugs,

Why Sexual Security Is Good For Your Well-being

you should be aware of the side effects those drugs might bring to your body. When one partner cannot participate in sexual intimacy due to drug abuse or other substances, the other spouse will suffer sexual deprivation. When you take care of your health and well-being, you are also doing it for your loved one. That is practicing unselfish love.

Under normal circumstances, the best sexual intimacy can be achieved when both partners are ready emotionally and physically to express this beautiful love-making relationship.

Our society and communities are plagued with sexual scandals. We read bad news about betrayals and misconducts every day in the media. For your romantic and sexual life to have a positive meaning, you must make a conscious deliberate decision to make sure you pursue true love to protect yourself from the common and ordinary way of life choices and protect those you love by remaining pure in your thoughts, words, and actions.

When you believe you are special, you will never behave below your standard of expectations. Those who maintain sexual purity are those who know they are special, noble, and holy. Joseph told Potiphar's wife, "I cannot sleep with you because you are somebody's wife and I honor my God." When you do not value yourself in the light of the Cross of Jesus, you devalue your worth by the decisions you make about yourself and other people. Sexuality is the most abused relationship in the human kingdom. Noble men and women will avoid hurting themselves and others with their sexuality.

Avoiding sexual immorality does not happen in a vacuum. Humans are sexual beings by nature, therefore, it is very easy to fall into sexual temptations when you are not careful in your daily interactions with the opposite sex, or when you fail to create boundaries in your relationships with others, at the workplace, home, church, and at social gatherings. Here are some guidelines:

The Romantic dimension

a. If married, go with your spouse to social events, like churches, parties, and entertainment venues. If single, keep a circle of trusted friends with you and be close to your family members. Avoid being a loner.

b. Create healthy physical boundaries between you and the opposite sex. Avoid tight hugs, touching, or rubbing your body on each other, holding hands, staring at others, and wearing suggestive attire. All the above should happen between couples, but not with those with whom you are not intending to be intimate.

c. Ladies should be aware that it is natural for a man to be sexually aroused when they see any part of a woman's body exposed. Even when you are attracted to a man, exposing your body to trap him is evil. You need a man to value you as a whole being, and not be attracted to just a part of your body. Therefore, decent attire in public is noble. We should be our brothers' keepers even in sexual matters. And if you are married, it is an honor to your spouse not to flirt with the opposite sex.

d. When you are not intending to be in a relationship with the opposite sex, avoid long conversations, going out together, getting favors, etc. In short, avoid bonding with them.

e. When married or engaged, assure your spouse of your devotion and love for them and avoid awkward relationships with men and women. Sit together at events and social gatherings. Even when you are not on good terms, keep a united front in public. Do not discuss marital difficulties with workmates and relatives, but seek professional help. Never air your disagreements in public.

Why Sexual Security Is Good For Your Well-being

Maintaining a loving relationship with your spouse can prevent sexual misconduct. Possessiveness and control mechanisms are evil to both partners. Couples need to develop a relationship environment where each one does not feel trapped. Freedom of association is healthy, if not abused.

Talking about sexual intimacy in vulgar language is an insult to the beauty of romantic love and sexual intercourse. Ignorance of the sanctity of love and sex is witnessed when you hear all the insults heaped onto human sexuality in all the languages in the world. Those who demean human sexuality are not aware that they are demeaning and belittling their own sexuality and nature. This is also a form of pornography. It belittles the sanctity of human sexual nature as created by God.

Sexual intercourse should never occur where love and affection has not been developed into marriage. Sex should always express love.

God created sexual human beings. We are not subject to our sexuality as every human is endowed with the power of choice. Choosing to use your body to glorify God means you honor your body by doing only that will make you and your spouse happy.

It is important to know how your sex drive works. There are some people with higher sexual drives than others. Recognizing your strengths and weaknesses as far as your sexuality is concerned is very crucial for morality in sexual matters. (1 Corinthians 7; 1-2). Make wise decisions that can protect your sexual well-being.

Walking The Narrow Way

ACKNOWLEDGING YOUR SEXUALITY and the pitfalls that can affect you and others should prompt one to create healthy boundaries between opposite sexes and seek to develop healthy relationships with others.

Avoid rubbing your body on others and instead, shake their hand, or wave to them. If you are the boss, set a dress code in the office and always maintain professionalism at the workplace. Sexuality should not be used as bait to exploit anyone's attention or as a threat for intimidation.

Avoid being with the opposite sex in private places alone and encourage group lunches. If you are a clergy member, make visitations with a third party and do counseling within the vicinity of others in sight.

Avoid looking at porn in all its many forms. Pornography is poison to a human being's sexual brain.

Learn how to take care of your body, mind, and spirit by meditation, exercise, and prayers.

Remind yourself that the person you are attracted to have a need for true love, and using them for your sexual desires is selfish and dangerous.

The Romantic dimension

Sexual purity begins with purity of thoughts. What you imagine, think, and watch in the media affects your reaction to sexuality.

Exercise regularly and participate in healthy conversations. Train your mind to see humans as people and not sexual objects.

If you are single, plan to get a wife or husband in order to be sexually fulfilled. Seeking a long-lasting relationship is one method to prevent sexual immorality.

1. If you do not want any relationship or have not found a spouse, find something meaningful to keep your energy and mind busy, and keep family and friends close to avoid loneliness. Attend religious services or volunteer to serve humanity. "An idle mind is the devil's workshop."

While single, read books that inform on love, family, and sexuality in positive ways, so that you can be prepared to love someone in the future.

Learn to fall in love with yourself before you try to love someone else. A healthy sense of your value as a human being is crucial to a heathy relationship with others.

Sexual intercourse is not meant for selfish gratification. Any time sex is presented as an act devoid of a relationship, then the human value is defiled and devalued.

It is very important to learn that every human being has other needs besides sexual fulfillment such as the need to bond, belong, and be loved.

Sexual desires cannot and will not be satisfied by multiple partners. The more sexual partners one seeks, the deeper the emptiness. Only Love fills the empty heart with joy.

Everyone needs to learn the responsibility that comes with sexual intimacy:

a. Every heart longs to belong to someone on a permanent basis.

b. Everyone needs to be loved as a whole person.

c. No human heart in their right senses wants to share sexual partners.

d. Every child needs and wants to be born to a couple who love and care for each other.

The mystery of Romantic Love, is that, while we accept to be loved by our parents who also love our siblings. The human heart can only accept to be loved and to love only one individual at a time as far as romantic love is concerned.

Therefore, one cannot claim to love their spouse at the same time have a sexual affair with another person.

Abstinence from sexual immorality comes from the belief that humans are a sacred creation of God. The human body should be treated with honor that brings happiness to both partners and honor to society.

Sexually transmitted diseases are spread due to people sleeping with multiple partners. Selfishness is the root cause of pain and suffering in the world. When you care about yourself and others, you will abstain from sexual immorality in all of its myriad of ugly forms.

Knowledge is power, but truth sets us free. It is crucial for parents to teach their children and young adults the beauty of sex and the many responsibilities that come with sexual intimacy. Some parents teach their children the dangers of sex only and so they set the stage for curiosity and so many young people get mixed ideas about sexuality. Even pregnancy is presented as a scare tactic.

Some parents cannot wait to teach their young adults how to prevent pregnancy by giving out contraceptives.

The Romantic dimension

Scare tactics or permissiveness does not solve the various problems of sexuality. Proper education on morality and responsibility is the way to go.

If you are not sure which way is the right way, seek to hear from the Author Himself–God the Creator of humanity.

God could have created Eve and just let her meet Adam on their own and figure out what was best for them. In His Wisdom, however, God introduced Adam to Eve and married them. He handed Adam the responsibility to care for Eve and she was created to meet Adam's needs. A man and a woman were created to meet each other's needs. (Hebrews 13; 4)

Everyone is born a sexual being. Sexuality should never be portrayed as something ugly or unpleasant. Neither should it be handled as something as simple as taking a bath. The truth is that sex is good at all times but wise people will not misuse it. Sex at the right age, with right person at the right time and place is in order. Just like no parent in their right mind can hand over a million dollars to a five year old to spend however they choose, sexual intimacy needs maturity of the mind, body, and intellect.

Human sexuality has been shrouded in secrecy and taboos for ages. The unclear principle has made it easy for ignorance about sexuality to spread like wildfire. I was told by a teenage girl in high school during sex education that a lot of girls in that school believed that if they waited to have sex until after the wedding, they would give birth to disabled kids. It is not hard for one to guess where that lie came from.

The clergy hardly ever talk about the beauty of human sexuality from the pulpit, except when they condemn adultery and fornication. Romantic love is also spurned by some as a childish topic. Ignorance about love and sexuality has made the devil happy and so many lives ruined.

There is so much advice from all corners on how to make marriage work. Yet, marriage will never work where love is sacrificed.

Unwanted pregnancies occur due to sex without love or commitment and disregard for human life. Millions if not billions of babies are aborted because of wrong policies on sexuality, economic convenience, or pure fear of shame. While animals hardly ever kill their young ones, this generation has abused the act of sex more than the previous ones. The lack of acknowledging the sanctity of our sexuality has ruined many lives including unborn children.

Those who view pornography in all its forms are known to harbor violence and sexual depravity. Whoever wants to keep their sanity should never start the habit.

Sexual misconduct is responsible for broken homes, loss of wealth, abandoned children, and even murders.

Sex is holy, and when humans mishandle holy things set aside by the Creator, the Designer of order and love, they separate themselves from the blessings of living a pure lifestyle. When you abandon principles that safeguard your wellbeing you actually chose to destroy your own life.

Those who seek good sex will look for true love and protect their relationships with their loved ones by all means possible.

It is important to note that no one can prevent sexual misconduct in a vacuum. One must deliberately choose to stay away from the other factors that contribute to sexual immorality such as:

a. Drugs and alcohol
b. Watching violent movies and pornography
c. Unhealthy eating habits and lack of physical activities
d. Immoral acquaintances
f. False teachings in some traditions and cultures.
g. Antisocial attitudes that impede proper interactions with people
h. Lack of self-control

Covenant Marriage

GOD MAKES COVENANTS with every relationship He forges with individuals. He made a covenant with Adam and Eve, Noah, Abraham and Abraham's descendants. Covenants are promises of faithfulness. God has always kept His promises as outlined in the Bible account. Marriage vows before God and men are a covenant promise where two love birds take an oath to love each other for better or for worse until death. Covenant marriage acknowledges God as the Founder and the Author of marriage.

A covenant marriage invokes the power of heaven and earth to protect each other from breaking vows made to each other, to God, and to humanity.

The vows made in the presence of God and man invoke death on the party who breaks the marriage covenant. Those who have experience divorce know the devastating pain and disappointment when a marriage covenant is broken.

God married the first couple in the Garden of Eden and set the process of leaving, cleaving, and becoming one flesh. Jesus said, 'What God has put together no man shall put asunder.' Matthew 19; 4-6

Breaking the covenant of marriage means parting with the guidelines the Creator laid down for marital union.

The Romantic Dimension

Disregard for Divine rules and guidelines causes separations and divorce.

Some couples do not want covenant marriages. They just want to live with each other with no promises. Love needs commitment. When there are no promises, there are no expectations.

The Author of marriage and family saw it fit to make covenants with humans as a binding promise of faithfulness. Humans should think about the seriousness of marital relationships as they affect the whole person as well as their offspring, relatives, and other people in general.

It is therefore very risky to be in a relationship to the level of living together with no binding or legal oath of commitment.

When God made a covenant with Adam, He took the responsibility to save humanity from the fall into sin and rebellion. And that promise was fulfilled when Jesus sacrificed His life by accepting death on the cross in order to heal humanity from the ravages of sin. Those who enter into this covenant promise, agree to keep their end of the bargain by obeying the natural and moral laws that govern life on planet earth as stipulated in the Bible. Those moral and natural laws include keeping marriage vows.

7. When you make a vow to love someone till death do you part, you pronounce life with each other and death without each other. Broken covenants can bring spiritual death to individuals involved. Before the break up of marriage, love has been strangled or betrayed. You can kill love by rejecting the principle of life. In other words the most reasons for which people break up for, are bad or evil things people do to each other. When we hurt people we actually reject the principle of love.

Traditional Marriages

These types of unions are the oldest in human history. The unions are sometimes determined by parents and in most cases with the approval of the couple. Traditional marriages mostly take place among individuals of the same race, tribe, and common belief systems.

Traditional marriages are the most common unions in the world. They are also the most successful due to environment and community support. The 'birds of the same feather flock together' principle works magic because of familiar expectations and order.

Common law marriages

This type of union is becoming popular in all parts of the world due to many reasons and circumstances such as:

a. Couples who do not want to spend fortunes on wedding ceremonies.
b. Couples whose relationship is opposed by parents or other relatives.
c. Couples who live together for financial gain or to spilt bills
d. Couples who do not want to commit to marriage vows.

Whatever method people choose to live together, one need to remember that only divine principles and vows can sustain relationships.

Whatever type of union a couple decides to enter into, there are always some kind of expectations. When the needs are not met, pain and disappointment is inevitable.

The Romantic Dimension

Covenant keepers.

The only one person whom we believe can never break His covenant with us is God. Many of us believe this because He is powerful and can make the impossible possible due to His nature. However, we all know humans are morally weak by nature, and to overcome their fallen nature every human needs the ability and power to make choices that can enable them to overcome the temptations that besets them. Love is the motivating power to overcome demons. That love is based on the Divine principle of action.

Acknowledging the moral weakness of human nature, many couples enter into marital relationships with fear of being betrayed by the person they love. This fear can be real or imagined. The fear of betrayal can paralyze one to the degree where they cannot fully love their spouse without reservations. A lot of those who have been betrayed before or have witnessed this phenomenon among friends and relatives can develop this fear. When in doubt, do not venture into romantic love relationships.

You cannot love fully when you harbor any kind of fear such as fear to fail, fear to succeed, or fear of not being loved. Love cannot exist where there is fear. Love drives out fear.

When someone loves you and you do not believe them, their love for you has no effect on you, because you must receive love for it to influence your decisions and actions. Therefore you should never be in a relationship when you do not believe you are loved by your lover.

When you go into a relationship with doubts and fears, you are not faithful to your feelings and at this stage. You are setting a stage for breaking a covenant. No one should start a relationship when in doubt.

When you claim to love someone, you need to be sure what that means. Your love ought to be genuine, dependable, and resilient. Covenant breakers are those who easily give up. Those who have no backbone to stand up for love and to protect their loved ones from unfaithfulness and betrayals have no business in romantic love.

Many couples think that as long as you are not married, it is no big deal breaking a relationship. While breaking marriage is never easy due to family and financial connections, breaking any marital love is still painful especially when one or both partners were in love for a long period of time. Being aware of the intricate and fragile nature of a human heart as far as romantic love is concerned, one ought to think deep about their decisions before allowing themselves to fall in Love. Both partners should think about the impact of their love to themselves, families, and friends. This step can reduce the number of break ups one will experience in their journey to love.

The greater the number of love partners you have, the more you become pessimist about love. Having dated several men or women exposes you to disappointments and disillusions about true love. It is wise to postpone dating after a break up in order to heal and ponder where you went wrong so you can make it right next time. Athletes do this all the time. They learn from their failure so that they do not repeat the mistakes of their past failures in sports.

When you are looking to marry a good wife be a good husband first so that you are able to choose a good wife. You cannot keep a good wife when you are not a good husband and vice versa.

Covenant breakers are those who expect others to be good when their actions are evil. When you want the world to have peace, you bring the peace to the world. Happy marriages begin with happy single people.

Failure can be an opportunity to start again. All successful people have failed before. Not everyone ends up with the first or the second person they fell in love with. However, the failed relationships should be lessons learned to do better and refine attitudes and beliefs. Romantic relationships are tricky due to the fact that success cannot be determined by one spouse.

The Romantic Dimension

The first and most important covenant is the one you make with yourself before you meet someone to love. Here are the reasons why:

a. You can decide never to harm yourself simply because someone might leave you.

b. You can swear to yourself that you will never be unfaithful even if your future spouse would betray you.

c. You can decide never to revenge. Revenge is for cowards who do not believe in themselves.

d. You can assure yourself that the next time you meet a new love, you will pour all your love on them with all you have.

e. You can determine that whoever falls in love with you cannot forget your love for them, and should they walk away you make sure they have been loved ultimately by you.

f. You can decide to learn to own up to your failures and mistakes and become big enough to apologize.

g. You can decide to be generous and kind even when your spouse is not.

h. You can learn how to be a good parent before you even think about being in a relationship

It might seem farfetched to make a covenant with oneself, but the belief that love just happens like lightening and that when in love you are helpless is dangerous and misleading. People choose to be in a relationship. Before that choice one needs to know what would be expected of them when they fall in love.

Romantic love needs foundation:

a. Spiritual direction – What does your spouse believe. Whom do they honor? What are their priorities?

b. Mental stability- Is your beloved dependable and rational and mentally heathy?

c. Emotional stability- How do they react in situations of disagreements and disappointments?

d. Financial management- How do they relate to money and wealth? Do they plan expenditures or are extravagant? Do they work hard or are lazy?

e. Cultural foundation- Does your spouse honor their parents? What is their cultural belief that would enhance your relationship? What would threaten your union?

Knowing someone's background is crucial to a marital union. Ask the right questions before you unite your life, body, and finances with someone you claim to love as romantic love cannot survive where there is no strong foundation.

Conflict Resolution

NO MATTER HOW loving a couple is, learning conflict resolution techniques is vital in order to maintain a safe environment for their love to grow and thrive. Love needs respect.

Honor is a virtue we learn from those who raised us, and also from God. When you honor your parents, teachers, and authority, you are capable of honoring your spouse. Honor is respect.

Respecting the opinion of your spouse can mean you disagree without being disagreeable. It means practicing gentility and kind mannerisms when there is a conflict of ideas, or decisions. Self-control is sacrificial love.

Honoring your spouse also means you desist from using explicit foul language and cursing when you do not get things to go your way. It also means that you do not intimidate, threaten, or consult other people to convince your spouse to agree with your opinion or ideas. You will desist from applying pressure to get your way. Gentility is refined love.

Postpone the discussion of sensitive issues when arguments start until such a time when both can calmly handle the issue. Or take a walk to get fresh air until your anger settles down. You cannot solve problems when you are angry. Meekness is silent love.

The Romantic dimension

Sometimes you need to sacrifice your own wants in order to win trust from your spouse. Trust is built over years and over the course of a relationship. Even when you are right, there will be times that you relinquish your rights for the sake of building and strengthening your relationship. Those who are always right will always be alone. Self-sacrifice is courageous love.

All relationships will encounter disagreements, but when your disagreements threaten your relationship, it is wise to seek professional marital counseling. Fools do not seek wisdom from others.

Badmouthing your spouse with your friends, relatives, and co-workers is a sure way to lose trust and worsen the disagreements. Character assassinations are for gossipers not problem solvers.

It might sound far-fetched, but the best time to pray for your spouse is when you do not see eye to eye on issues. Pray that God may give you wisdom to be loving when it is difficult to do so.

One of the best tactics to solve issues is to make time and sit at the table to discuss them. Before the discussion, set rules on how you both want to handle the meeting. For example, both of you to agree that there will be:

a) No yelling, no cursing

b) No banging table

c) No cutting each other off at mid-sentence

d) No bringing up past mistakes which are not related to the issue at hand. No bringing up issues which have already been agreed upon and solved.

e) Listening to each other and making sure you understand what your spouse meant to say.

In other words, couples need family meetings where ideas, decisions, and agreements are made like the ones we conduct or attend in our workplaces.

A couple's love life depends on how they manage their disagreements and solve their problems. The secret is to make sure they remain true and faithful to each other no matter the challenges.

Both partners ought to compromise their own wishes for each other to reach agreements and solve issues.

Unfaithfulness

INFIDELITY IS A sign of a spiritual problem. The couple needs to consult marital and sexual therapists. Their spiritual belief system ought to be assessed. When someone stands for nothing and believes nothing except their own selfish gratifications, they become dangerous to their family members and to society. The fact that infidelity is common everywhere today does not make it right no matter the explanation. A spouse and children feel betrayed by the one they love and trust. Parents feel the pain when their daughters or sons are betrayed by their spouses.

The one who breaks the vow or a promise to their loved ones also hurts themselves. Philandering does not bring peace of mind or happiness to the offender. The guilty are afraid. Living in fear and guilt is the worst emotional prison anyone would want to put themselves in. The offender also needs healing to lead a normal life again. This is possible when repentance and forgiveness occurs.

The victims of philandering spouses always feel something is wrong with them. They go through a low self-esteem period and sometimes do the same thing to prove someone can actually love them, admire them, and respect them. Or they could even try to harm themselves in various ways, or perhaps harm the offender. Because betrayal is so

The Romantic Dimension

painful and can cause mental breakdowns, both individuals need to seek treatments and spiritual counselling.

Most cheating spouses have some personal issues with a low esteem value of themselves, and false assessments of how to get away with cheating. Even when your spouse does not know you are cheating on them, your guilt torments you all the time. When you continue on the path of philandering, sooner or later you destroy your career, your reputation, and eventually you will almost certainly lose your family. There is no winning when it comes to betraying loved ones. The only way out of this all too common ordinary behavior is to seek help.

The offender must understand that their spouse can forgive them but decide to end the relationship. That is still forgiveness. The victim should also know that forgiveness does not mean to excuse the offence, but forgiveness brings healing to both partners whether they decide to continue with the relationship or not. Letting go of hurt and betrayal is not easy and does not happen instantly. Time is a crucial factor for healing.

Forgiveness gives us energy to live again. Even the children ought to forgive their cheating parents in order to be healed. The offender needs to forgive themselves too in order to live a fresh, clean life beyond their past.

Sexual misconduct, drug addiction, gambling, alcoholism, and domestic violence are major love breakers.

The addict needs to seek help to save themselves from early death and from losing their family.

The victims ought to remove themselves from an abusive environment and seek refuge to save themselves and the children involved. Living in an abusive relationship is *not* loving the abuser. The victim becomes an enabler. When you enable someone to keep doing evil, you are equally guilty.

No woman in her right mind should ever tolerate domestic violence. There is a lie women can tell themselves that, "He will change if I behave" or "all marriages have issues." Any time a spouse hits or verbally abuses you, you need to seek help. Self-respect and healthy self-esteem are very important before one enters into a relationship. When you allow someone to abuse you, it is because you do not value yourself. You must believe that your life as an individual is more important than the marriage. You should love enough to let go.

Love is under assault from many forces of evil. It is a battle of faith to maintain love and to recover it from the pitfalls of life.

Lack of integrity cannot be confined to sexual misconduct only. Sexual infidelity is the last stroke. But before philandering and cheating, there are so many other incidents of negligence such as:

a. When a couple fails to spend time together, they create loneliness and distractions from each other.

b. Couples who keep secrets from each other create distrust.

c. Unresolved conflicts create resentments.

d. Failure to provide for the family can be neglect and abuse of the role of a husband.

e. Deliberate withholding of sexual intimacy is unfaithfulness.

f. When one partner assumes the authority to have the last word in all decisions, it makes the other feel trapped in a bad relationship and feel insignificant

g. Laziness and passivity on important issues could be perceived as neglecting your spouse's needs.

The Romantic dimension

3. Every love has mountains to climb. There is no one who can testify that their relationship has not encountered minor or major challenges that threaten the existence of their love. When you love someone, you will do your best to solve issues. Selfishness is clinging to something that hurts your spouse.

Breakups

BREAKING UP A relationship can be painful and disastrous. When there is a mutual agreement on ending a short-term marital relationship that did not involve sex, the disappointment is not as painful as those who became intimate or were in a longtime relationship. Most people do not marry the first person they loved or thought they did. Therefore, the majority of people have experienced break ups of some kind for various reasons. Some break ups have less drama, but some are melodramatic and can even be lethal.

Divorce is one of the most disastrous breakups and can tear one's heart into pieces. Few people survive the effects of divorce like loss of career, wealth, and even health. The most devastating effect of divorce on an individual is the disillusionment with the idea of love itself. Few are able to fully love another person again after divorce.

Divorce harms children in more ways than adults. The children cannot replace their parents, while parents can replace their spouses. The act of insanity of revenge with which a divorcing couple handle the break up can destroy the well-being of their children emotionally, spiritually, and mentally. But the divorcing parents can lessen the damage by being civil and polite to each other during and after divorce.

The Romantic Dimension

Children of divorced parents need therapy just like adults. The parents ought to agree on how to maintain a nurturing environment that will accommodate the financial, academic, and mental well-being of their children.

a. The divorcing parents ought to put the interests of their children as a priority over their disagreements.

b. The divorcing parents must resist the temptation to talk ill of their ex-spouse to the children.

c. The parents should resist to use the children as a bait and a weapon against their ex-spouse.

d. The parents must sacrifice their own individual wants and needs and take care of their children

e. The parents ought to postpone dating until they make sure their children are ready to handle the introduction of a new person to their space. It takes time for children to learn that the new woman or man is not replacing their parent.

The parents ought to include the interests of their children when they decide to date again. The new date should be a person who comes with full knowledge of your responsibility for your children.

f. The parents should keep respectful communication with their former spouse for the sanity of their children. Open resentment in the presence of your children is toxic to their young brains.

Revenge between divorcing couples is the most costly habit that unwise couples engage in during breakups. Couples will save lawyers' fees and the cost of wealth settlements when they decide to settle everything with mutual understanding.

a. Revenge does not help one heal from the heartbreak of a breakup. By stark contrast, forgiveness can heal both partners in the long run.

b. Shaming your ex-spouse says a lot about you and not about them.

c. Bitterness and animosity destroy the health of an individual.

d. Forgiveness and letting go is the only way for one to find peace after a break up. (Matthew 6:14)

One's ability and willingness to forgive the wrongs done in the past is nobility of character. It is possible to be a better future spouse to someone else when there are no grudges held within the heart.

It is important to acknowledge contributions to the break up. "It takes two to tango." When you always believe that others are wrong and you are right, then you will never change what is wrong with your own attitude or actions.

When you vow to never forgive someone, you actually take the oath of self-destruction. Forgiving the people who hurt you in the past is a process to living again. The more you keep repeating the ills done the more you poison your inner beauty, outer appearance, and retard your own progress in everything you do. The Lord says 'vengeance in mine' (Romans 12; 19). Remember no one gets away with evil. Evil has a way to destroy its victim. The common term "I will not go down without a fight" is a misplaced term in interpersonal relationships.

Love Companionship

WHEN YOU LOVE someone you must take note that Romantic Love needs foundation.

You need someone who is a friend and a companion.

Some relationships suffer due to failure of one or both partners' investment of quality and quantity time together. No matter how deep your love for each other is, spending time together is a solid foundation for love to grow and mature

You need someone who cheers for your success and brings the best out of you.

Another reason for relationship failure is when your spouse becomes your competitor. Some men feel their wives or girlfriends should not earn more money than them or get a higher education than them. And some get intimidated as their partners climb the ladder of success in their careers or political aspirations. Love will automatically be sacrificed when you become jealous of your partner. True love wants the best for the other person.

You need someone who will work hard and make your life with them less of a burden. The reason we get married is not just for love. We need someone who is not a burden but a companion in all aspects of our relationship. When the husband makes money, the

The Romantic Dimension

wife should have ideas of how to do investments and not focus on spending. A wife and children need a husband and father who will think about their financial well-being when he will not be present in their lives. A wise father and husband will not get involved in illegal practices to earn money or be in illicit relationships as both practices would harm the family. That is true love.

Some of the practices that harm the family where money is involved are

a) Gambling, alcoholism, and laziness

b) Living beyond your income and acquisition of unnecessary debts.

c) Buying stuff you do not need in competition with your neighbors

d) Investing in Ponzi schemes with the promise to get rich quick.

e) Investing your resources where you cannot supervise or enjoy the proceeds. In other words, unwise investments can harm your family.

Pleasure before work is a dangerous attitude. Those who constantly seek the lure of entertainment over hard work and financial savings are at risk of failure to keep a spouse or maintain a family. Balance between work, leisure, and savings is very crucial in the modern day lifestyle. It is wise to learn personal financial management no matter how small or large your income is. This would save many relationships from break ups and divorce. It is very important to note that those who earn a good amount of money are more likely to be in debt than those individuals with limited income. So, it is true that it is not how much you earn but how you plan your expenditures.

Selfish love is when you want to have both worlds without making any sacrifices. When your love is genuine, you must learn to be able to care for another human being by sacrificing time, money, and anything that threatens your relationship with each other. Sometimes you will be required to sacrifice, even your best friends or relatives in order to maintain your marriage.

Love and Faith

LIFE IS FULL of uncertainties. Love is always the victim of challenges. There are dark forces beyond human powers. These dark forces' main agenda is to stifle love and promote pessimism. When you meet a couple who have been married for many years and still vow to love each other, they will tell you stories about the dark forces they had to overcome in order to be together. Therefore, it is one thing to be faithful and devoted to each other, and it is another thing to overcome the dark forces.

These are some of the symptoms of dark forces in operation:

1. Each time something beyond your control threatens to break your relationships, dark forces are involved. Examples are diseases that can kill your spouse, natural disasters, jail terms political upheavals and incarcerations, civil and international wars. Immigration issues and poverty can wreak havoc on your love life.

We need faith in the Divine power to help us overcome these forces or survive the attack. God in His word promises to be with us in all circumstances. If there is love, God is that Love.

2. Ignorance; The saying 'What you do not know cannot harm you' is a truth laced with poison. Ignorance can be a sin. When you are ignorant, you are a danger to yourself and a danger to others, obliviously.

When someone breaks the known law, they at least want to find ways to escape the consequences of breaking that particular law. But when someone breaks unknown natural laws unconsciously they become a weapon in the hands of dark forces. The natural consequences of breaking the natural laws flow over to the whole community and to the whole world at large

Examples; Polygamy and forced marriages do not promote love relationships. Young girl's careers and education cut short due to ignorant parents. Children born in the confusing relationship environment will repeat the same cycle and the community will remain in the vicious circle of ignorance.

Ignorance about sex and love plague the masses today. Sex has taken center stage over love and commitment and the modern media has not helped much but has unconsciously promoted sex over love. This ignorance is very costly to all relationships. Sex has been portrayed as an act of passion and lust rather than an act emanating from deep feelings of love and commitment to the beloved. Sex is hardly portrayed as an expression of love even in secular movies, lust seems to win the day.

How you write your love story will impact others positively or negatively. It is my hope that we can learn the art of loving a human being when we are given space and chance.

Life in general has many challenges that time and space would not allow me to mention them all. However love, peace, and forgiveness can help overcome some challenges many couples face.

Love And Faith

In order to live fully, we must focus on the beauty of love, sex laughter, friendship, and family. In order to triumph over evil, we must promote love because love will win at the end of everything.

When you begin to love you begin to fully live.

CPSIA information can be obtained
at www.ICGtesting.com
Printed in the USA
LVHW021135111121
702940LV00008B/440